# IMAGES OF WAR SPECIAL

# T-34

*The Red Army's Legendary Medium Tank*

## RARE PHOTOGRAPHS FROM WARTIME ARCHIVES

## Anthony Tucker-Jones

*Illustrated by*
**David Lee Hemingway**

Pen & Sword
**MILITARY**

First published in Great Britain in 2015 by
PEN & SWORD MILITARY
an imprint of
Pen & Sword Books Ltd,
47 Church Street,
Barnsley,
South Yorkshire
S70 2AS

ISBN 978 178159 095 9

Typeset by CHIC GRAPHICS

Printed and bound in Malta by Gutenberg Press Ltd

Pen & Sword Books Ltd incorporates the imprints of Pen & Sword
Archaeology, Atlas, Aviation, Battleground, Discovery, Family History, History,
Maritime, Military, Naval, Politics, Railways, Select, Social History, Transport,
True Crime, and Claymore Press, Frontline Books, Leo Cooper, Praetorian
Press, Remember When, Seaforth Publishing and Wharncliffe.

*For a complete list of Pen & Sword titles please contact*
Pen & Sword Books Limited
47 Church Street, Barnsley, South Yorkshire, S70 2AS, England
E-mail: enquiries@pen-and-sword.co.uk
Website: www.pen-and-sword.co.uk

# Contents

Introduction: A War Winner ................................................ 5

Acknowledgements ........................................................ 8

Prologue: Grievous Casualties ............................................ 9

Chapter One
**Birth of a War Winner – T-34/76** ..................................... 13

Chapter Two
**A Winning Upgrade – T-34/85** ........................................ 29

Chapter Three
**T-34 Variants** ....................................................... 45

Chapter Four
**Too Few Too Late** .................................................... 57

Chapter Five
**Moscow Miracle** ...................................................... 69

Chapter Six
**T-34s in Ukraine** .................................................... 81

Chapter Seven
**T-34s in White Russia** ............................................... 91

Chapter Eight

**T-34s on the Seelow Heights** .................................................. **103**

Chapter Nine

**T-34 Tank Aces** ............................................................ **111**

Chapter Ten

**T-34 Killers** ............................................................... **121**

Chapter Eleven

**Cold War T-34s** ............................................................ **133**


**Epilogue: Koshkin versus Kotin** ............................................ **141**

**Further Reading** ........................................................... **144**

# Introduction
# A War Winner

When Pen & Sword approached me about producing a pictorial history of the T-34 tank I immediately faced a dilemma: what is there to say about this superb Soviet-designed tank that has not already been said many times before? Then it struck me: the T-34 is the one weapon that truly won the Second World War. A bold statement I grant you, but when one considers the vastness of the Eastern Front the campaigns fought in France, Italy and North Africa and, indeed, in the Far East were just sideshows when it came to armoured warfare. Throughout the Second World War tank designs came and went, but the T-34 was the one constant from 1940 to 1945. After Hitler's invasion of Russia the T-34 became the spearhead of the Red Army's blitzkrieg that took it from Stalingrad and Kursk to the very heart of Berlin and victory over the Nazis.

Following the German invasion the Red Army floundered around, its forces in disarray no matter how many counterattacks it launched. Fortunately, though, its tank factories had been saved, which meant the T-34 began appearing in ever-greater numbers. Then, at the end of 1942, the Red Army's new tank armies, equipped with the T-34, played a key role in shattering the German, Italian, Hungarian and Romanian lines at Stalingrad. The following summer the T-34 sent Hitler's panzers reeling at Kursk.

Designing a tank is a simple compromise between speed, weight, armour and armament. Get the combination right and it gives you a winning edge; get it wrong and it ends in disaster. Most early Soviet tanks opted for speed as they were regarded as little more than armoured cavalry designed to charge through the enemy's lines in support of the infantry. The dominance of cavalry officers in the Red Army after the Russian Civil War was largely responsible for this mindset. At the same time the Red Army was struggling to learn the most effective ways to employ their ever-growing numbers of tanks. In the summer of 1941 all of Russia's light, medium and heavy tank designs proved an unmitigated disaster in the face of Hitler's panzers and superior German strategy. Only after a very shaky start did one new tank catch the eye of the Red Army's generals – the T-34/76. It also caught the eye of the German generals.

While the T-34 had a number of innovative design advantages over its competitors, one in particular stands out. The critical problem faced by the British Churchill and Cromwell, the American Sherman and the German Panzer Mk IV and Panther was that they could not be upgunned beyond a 76mm/77mm calibre gun. The hulls of these tanks would simply not permit a larger turret and therefore a larger anti-tank gun. This greatly limited their tank-killing capabilities. The Allies never really overcame this shortcoming until the advent of the Pershing tank armed with a 90mm gun and by then the war was all but over. The Germans got round this limitation by producing higher-velocity 75mm guns and the Tiger I and II armed with an 88mm gun, but the Tigers were only made in relatively limited numbers.

In contrast, the squat hull of the T-34/76 enabled the Soviets to conduct a significant enhancement by the simple expedient of fitting a much larger cast turret that could house a much bigger gun – namely an 85mm high-velocity anti-aircraft gun redesigned as an anti-tank weapon. The resulting T-34/85 may not have given the Red Army battlefield dominance, but it certainly gave them much-needed parity with the later panzers. This, coupled with the T-34's vast numbers, was a war-winning combination. The T-34's design ensured that not only was it easy to build but, just as importantly, it was easy to maintain on the battlefield regardless of the weather.

While the Allies and the Germans enjoyed success with a range of tank destroyers and assault guns, those T-34s converted to the assault gun role proved far less satisfactory. The British and Americans armed some Shermans with 76mm and 77mm guns, but these were very few in number and did not make up for the Sherman's poor armour. Likewise the Sherman-based Achilles/Wolverine tank destroyer faced the same problem. It was in trying to replicate the German *Sturmgeschütz* or assault gun concept that the T-34 came a cropper, its tank-destroyer variants proving little more than a stopgap until the heavy KV tank chassis married to a 152mm howitzer produced a really invincible tank killer. Only the T-34-based SU-100 tank destroyer provided the additional punch that the T-34/85 lacked.

It was Soviet experiences in Spain that led indirectly to the T-34's development, which eventually gave them an important technological edge over the Germans. In the wake of the Spanish Civil War many experts concluded that the anti-tank gun was more effective than the tank, and the rudimentary mechanised combat in Spain refuted the new theories about mechanised warfare. They failed to take into account the unsuitable terrain, the poorly trained crews and the relatively small numbers of tanks employed.

General Dimitri Pavlov, a Soviet tank specialist who served in Spain and was one of the innovators of Soviet mechanisation during the early 1930s, had observed the increased use and accuracy of anti-tank weapons. Both the BT-5 and T-26 suffered a gradual reduction in armour effectiveness and this led the Soviet Union to ensure that its tanks not only were resistant to shell splinters and small arms, but could also withstand direct hits from small-calibre artillery.

Ironically, Pavlov's experiences in Spain would ultimately cost him his life, for he drew the wrong conclusions about the deployment of armour. He advocated the French doctrine whereby tanks were used in direct support of the infantry. He felt that the doctrine of blitzkrieg by mass armour was not sound. On returning to Russia in 1939, he argued in favour of disbanding the unwieldy Soviet tank corps.

Just months before Hitler's attack, senior Soviet commanders attended a key conference followed by war games during December 1940 and January 1941. There was then a gathering in the Kremlin, the last of its sort before the German invasion. The aim was to assess the progress made by the armed forces following the war with Finland and Hitler's blitzkrieg victories in Europe. Some commanders still advocated the horse over the tank and crucially Stalin, while he defended the tank, made no executive decision about the future of the Soviet armoured forces.

General la N. Fedorenko warned that there were 'too few modern tanks and that a number of tanks which were standard equipment in the Red Army were already obsolete'. He argued that no time should be lost in increasing production of the new T-34 and KV tanks and that funding should be redirected to this end. Marshal Grigory Ivanovic Kulik, who favoured cavalry and artillery, was dismissive and Stalin stood up and said that the balance was right. Crucially, the chance to crank up T-34 production was lost. Nonetheless some 55,000 T-34s were eventually built, representing 68 per cent of Soviet tank production during the Second World War.

# Acknowledgements

Once again I am deeply indebted to my good friend Preston Isaac, the proprietor of the superb Cobbaton Combat Collection, who allowed me to experience at first hand and photograph in minute detail his fully functioning Model 1945 T-34/85. This enabled me to sample the privations and complete lack of creature comforts endured by T-34 tank crews. The driving and fighting compartments, as in all tanks, are little more than steel prison cells full of sharp-edged hazards to catch out the unwary – the crews wore padded tanker's helmets for good reason. On top of this there is an unrelenting stink of diesel emanating from the fuel tank and the engine, as well as grease and oil on every surface. Add this to the inevitable odour of the unwashed crew and it must have been a heady mixture.

Under way, the T-34 is a very noisy, roaring, clanking monster that belches smoke and dispenses death and destruction in its path. It is certainly not a creation to get too starry-eyed about. With the hatches battened down, one can imagine the sense of sheer terror the crew must have endured every time an enemy round clanged loudly on the outside of the hull. Relief that they were still alive must have been followed by frantic activity as they fired back at their tormentors as quickly as possible.

## Photograph Sources[*]

My thanks to author, journalist and photographer Tina Orr Munro who kindly assisted with the Cobbaton Combat Collection photo-shoot and provided the very detailed exterior and interior technical shots. Also thanks to Scott Pick, who assisted with images from his comprehensive Eastern Front Collection and likewise Russian military expert Nik Cornish, who runs the first-class Stavka picture library. The latter tracked down photographs of some of the more unusual T-34 variants.

---

[*] Publisher's note: some of the photographs in this book have previously appeared in the author's *Armoured Warfare* series but in light of their quality the publisher felt it worthwhile to include them in this volume specifically on the T-34.

# Prologue
# Grievous Casualties

A team of talented designers under Zh. Y. Kotin developed the KV heavy tank, and another under M.I. Koshkin, A.A. Morozov and N.A. Kucherenko developed the famous T-34 medium tank. Engine-builders created the powerful V-2 diesel engine for the tanks. The KV and T-34 were the best tanks built before the war. . . . The task on the eve of the war, however, was to organise their mass production as soon as possible.

Marshal Georgi Zhukov

The T-34 almost never saw the light of day thanks to the infighting and political rivalries amongst the Soviet Union's generals, tank designers, factory managers and politicians. In an act of unprecedented bravado, the T-34's lead designer Mikhail Koshkin endangered his health and ultimately sacrificed his life to prove the tank's abilities. Ironically, the T-34 was not even the official or proffered new medium tank design – it was Koshkin who went out on a professional limb and suggested an alternative to the prototype designs that were already under consideration. By personally presenting it to Stalin, he sidestepped all the nay-sayers and the crucial decision was made.

At the same time those overseeing the construction of the Red Army's latest KV-1 heavy tank, along with the Soviet artillery directorate (responsible for producing anti-tank guns), did all they could to hinder and delay the birth of the T-34. The rivalry between the tank-manufacturing plants in Leningrad and Kharkov ensured that there was an ugly tug of war over resources and priorities. Although everything was done to safeguard the future of the KV-1 after the opening months of the Nazi invasion, it was the T-34 that was kept in production. Both factories had to be relocated once Leningrad was besieged and Kharkov overrun by the Wehrmacht. The new home for the T-34 became known, aptly enough, as Tankograd.

Long before all this, Joseph Stalin's actions to secure his power base by purging his rivals almost robbed the Soviet Union of the T-34 altogether. Stalin was firmly in control by 1929 and had no intention of relinquishing it. Within two years, fearing the influence of his exiled arch-rival Leon Trotsky (the number two figure, after Lenin, during the 1917 Bolshevik revolution), he turned his attentions to the Red Army. This was one of the first purges of the armed forces, and it proved minor and bloodless. Those involved could count themselves extremely lucky for they were simply removed from post and in many cases dismissed. Relatively painlessly, Stalin promoted his old Russian Civil War cronies.

Trying to haul the Soviet Union into the twentieth century by its bootstraps, Stalin launched his first 'Five Year Plan' in 1928. Its goal was to industrialise an agricultural economy largely trapped in the Middle Ages. The Red Army was also to be modernised. Mechanisation required technical knowhow and that posed a problem. There was a shortage of designers and to get round this the Red Army cherry-picked young engineers from the Soviet automotive industry in 1927 to be trained in tank design. This was fortuitous, for just two years later the Red Army General Staff issued a special directive giving priority to the production of tanks. Under Mikhail Tukhachevsky's reform programme this called for tankettes to conduct reconnaissance; light tanks to act as cavalry; medium tanks to force the breakthrough; and heavy tanks to subdue fortified areas. By that stage the Soviets only had the T-18 in production; this was based on the M-17, which had been produced during the Russian Civil War.

In the summer of 1929 a series of tractor and car plants were set up in Moscow, Gorkiy, Stalingrad, Chelyabinsk and Yaroslavl. These would be the basis for the Soviet Union's wartime tank industry. The Second 'Five Year Plan' launched in 1932 saw Stalin turn his attention on the hapless *kulaks* (wealthy peasants) for he wished to collectivise their farms, which meant appropriating their land. It has been estimated that by 1936 seven million people had died in the collectivisation famine and deportations.

Tukhachevsky was a modern thinker who appreciated the concepts of modern mechanised warfare. In the mid-1930s he had expanded his tactical concept of 'Deep Battle' to a larger strategic concept known as 'Deep Operation'. This bore a striking resemblance to the Nazi blitzkrieg as it envisaged multiple penetrations of the enemy's front with exploitations of over 60 miles in depth using modern weapons such as tanks and aircraft.

Military vehicles were delivered to the Red Army at a rate previously unknown and it soon had approximately as many tanks as France – which at the time was the pre-eminent European power. By 1935 Stalin had 10,000 tanks. At the same time he began to fear that a revived and powerful Red Army would pose a threat to him. Stalin turned to the Peoples' Commissariat of Internal Affairs – the dreaded NKVD, which came into being in 1934 as the forerunner of the KGB. Three years later the Great Purge (*Ezhovschina*) fell upon the Red Army with a vengeance, leaving it in a state of almost total disarray. Among the victims was Tukhachevsky, whose ideas were discredited by vengeful rivals. It was against this background that the T-34 was designed, developed and put into production – under such circumstances it was little short of a miracle. West of Moscow the Nazis discovered exactly what that miracle was. General Heinz Guderian commented:

On October 6th 1941 our headquarters was moved forward to Sevsk. 4th Panzer Division was attacked by Russian tanks to the south of Mzensk [Mtensk] and went through some bad hours. This was the first occasion on which the vast superiority of the Russian T-34 to our tanks became plainly apparent. The division suffered grievous casualties.

Mikhail Koshkin's A-34 prototype. Koshkin felt that the proposed A-20/30 designs did not meet the Red Army's requirements, nor would they be easy to mass produce. The A-34 bears a striking resemblance to the subsequent T-34 Model 1940.

# Chapter One

# Birth of a War Winner – T-34/76

Ironically it was a much-modified American tank design that indirectly gave rise to the birth of the T-34. Certainly very few features on the T-34 were original, as most of them had already appeared in one shape or another on earlier Soviet or foreign tanks. However, it was the right combination in one vehicle that was the great achievement of a young Soviet engineer by the name of Mikhail Koshkin and his team.

Koshkin was sent to the Kharkov Locomotive Factory (also known as the Komintern Factory) in Ukraine in 1936. The factory's design bureau had been involved in modernising the BT fast tank and was under instruction to design a new medium tank, designated the A20, utilising the BT's dual wheel/track facility. Alexander Morozov, who had designed the new V-2 diesel engine, was responsible for the power train; Nikolai Kucherenko and P. Vasihev led the suspension team, while M. Tarshinov was responsible for the armour.

Koshkin must have been uneasy about his appointment as head of the Kharkov design bureau. The vacancy had only come about because Comrade A. Firsov and many of his team responsible for the BT tank programme had been arrested following one of Stalin's purges. Koshkin and his colleagues were also faced by the deeply entrenched vested interests of the other factories producing light and heavy tanks for the Red Army. In particular, the tank design bureau in Leningrad sought favour with Kliment Voroshilov, the Defence Commissar, by eventually naming their heavy tank the KV. Ironically Koshkin had started his career in Leningrad.

The draft design for the first Soviet 'shell-proof' tank, with greatly inclined armour, armed with a 45mm gun and weighing 17.7 tons, was completed in November 1937. General Dmitri Pavlov, head of the Directorate of Armoured Forces, wanted Soviet tanks to be shell-proof, specifically against the 37mm anti-tank gun. Likewise the engine needed updating as the petrol engine in service had a habit of catching fire; what was needed was a diesel engine with a low flashpoint.

Ironically, although General Pavlov concluded – wrongly – from the Spanish Civil War that massed armour was ineffective, he was in part responsible for the genesis of the T-34. Although he consigned the Red Army's tanks to an infantry support role (which spelt disaster in 1941), he at least helped provide a tank that would ensure final victory.

The Spanish Civil War had shown that the anti-tank weapon had dominance over the tank on the battlefield. Making a tank shell-proof involved not only safeguarding it from small arms fire and shell splinters, but also from small-calibre artillery and anti-tank weapons. What the Red Army needed, in light of the performance of the Soviet BT-7 and T-26 tanks in Spain, was a tank that could withstand a shell from a 37mm anti-tank gun at any range and from a 76mm gun at 1,000m. Initial improvements were achieved by upgrading the BT-7.

The Soviet BT fast tank was a copy of the American Christie and the modernised version replaced the modified Soviet aero tank engine with a V-2 diesel unit that had been developed specifically for use in tanks. This gave increased range, cut down on maintenance and, crucially, offered better cold weather performance. The crews were doubtless happy with the change to diesel, it being less flammable than petrol. Another upgrade to the BT-7M, which would later be reflected in the T-34, was improved shot deflection achieved by replacing the boat-shaped hull front with an angled, sloping nose plate. A hull gun was also fitted, together with a 76.2mm partially stabilised turret gun.

The BT-7M was followed by the experimental BT-IS (investigator tank), which was fitted with sloping hull sides that extended over the top of the tracks to the full width of the vehicle. A sloping turret was also fitted. Both the BT-7M and the BT-IS greatly influenced the A20, which also had a sloped hull and retained the BT's feature of being able to run on either the tracks or the road-wheels. This option, however, greatly increased the weight of the tank and caused difficulties in mass production and maintenance.

Koshkin and Morozov presented a wooden mock-up of the A-20 to the Defence Council of the Soviet Peoples' Commissars in May 1938. Neither man was enthusiastic about the dual wheel/track capability. Koshkin had concluded that the Red Army seldom used the BT tank in the wheeled mode, which imposed severe design difficulties and weight problems on the manufacturers. Russia's roads were such that being able to run the tank on just its wheels did not really offer any great advantages. Likewise during combat the crews were unlikely to bother changing the tracks to suit the conditions.

During a presentation to Stalin, the designers reasoned that the new tank needed at least 30mm of armour and a 76.2mm gun rather than the current standard 45mm tank gun. Crucially, though, the A20 turret could not take a larger-calibre weapon. This led to an enlarged design known as the A30, to be armed with a 76.2mm gun. Koshkin also pressed his case for abandoning the dual wheel/track feature, suggesting the A-32 would run only on tracks, which meant the armour could be increased to 60mm.

While Stalin seems to have been content to take advice from his experts, he cannot have been greatly encouraged by the Red Army's existing medium and heavy tank designs. The multi-turreted T-35 heavy tank was a lumbering 50-ton monster and only sixty had been built. The Red Army's only medium tank, the multi-turreted T-28, looked more like a heavy tank and was just as unwieldy.

As a result Koshkin and the Kharkov design team found themselves developing not one tank but three: the A-20, the A-30 and the A-32. The A-30 was quickly abandoned because its A20 turret could not take a larger weapon. But although the Soviet high command had accepted Koshkin's proposal for the A-32 and authorised a prototype, they had not given up on the A-20. Both prototypes were completed at Kharkov at the beginning of 1939 and were subsequently displayed to the Armoured Directorate. The latter recommended the increase in armour on the A-32 and the more powerful gun, in accordance with Pavlov's wishes.

Fortunately for the Red Army it already had a 76.2mm weapon in the form of the USV-39 (in later modification the ZiS-3) designed by Vasiliy Grabin. The Model 1936 and Model 1939 were the standard divisional field guns.* General B.L. Vannikov, head of Soviet armaments, was fulsome in his praise of this weapon:

> The tank variant of the ZiS gun considerably outclassed the German tank guns in firing range and penetrating ability. The combination of a number of good tactical and technical qualities of the ZiS gun (light weight, small dimensions, convenience in operation, etc.) made it possible to outstrip the Germans and to design the T-34 tank with a 76mm calibre gun which had a high armour-piercing capability and good accuracy over great distances.

There was some discussion about arming the T-34 with an even larger gun. Marshal Kulik, head of the Main Artillery Directorate, suggested a 107mm weapon; this won approval with Stalin, who was familiar with a First World War field gun of similar size. In theory this would have been a war winner; in reality it was nonsense. Vannikov was aghast; such a tank gun did not exist and if it did it would need a much bigger turret. As a first step he suggested it would be simpler to increase the muzzle velocity of the 76mm gun and then progress to an 85mm gun. Kulik was of the opinion that

---

* The Model 1936 (F-22) was a flawed dual-role field and anti-aircraft gun. The lack of 360° traverse meant it was not used in the anti-aircraft role and as a field piece it was too heavy. The Model 1939 (USV) was a much better proposition but this was replaced by the much more durable and accurate Model 1942 (ZiS-3), which was simpler and cheaper to produce. Development of the ZiS-3 was kept hidden from Marshal Grigory Ivanovich Kulik, head of the Main Artillery Directorate, for fear he would refuse to approve it.

This photo shows (*from left to right*) the clear evolution of the BT-7M through the A-20 and T-34 Model 1940 to the T-34 Model 1941. This development reflected Koshkin's proposals that the tank should only run on very wide tracks and that the sloped armour should be increased, along with the size of the gun.

(*Opposite, top*) The initial T-34 Model 1940 entered full-scale production in the autumn of 1940. It is recognisable by the rolled plate turret and the distinctive short L-11 76.2mm gun mounted in a cast cradle welded to a flush outside mantle. It also had a large single hatch, seen here in the open position.

(*Opposite, below*) A T-34 Model 1940 with the cast turret designed by V. Buslov and V. Nitsenko. Easier to produce than the initial rolled plate welded type, these cast turrets were produced at Gorkiy. They retained the single turret hatch.

tanks were a waste of time, as the artillery would simply knock them out. At every stage he opposed giving tank production a greater share of resources. Vannikov's dogged opposition to Kulik resulted in him being arrested and imprisoned just before Hitler's invasion of the Soviet Union. Subsequently Stalin had the good sense to release and reappoint him.

On the eve of the Second World War in 1939 the A-32 prototype was extensively trialled, which led to modifications to the transmission. This final redesign by Koshkin's team was known as Project T-34; it ran only on tracks, using the clutch and transmission brake system of steering. The suspension consisted of large distinctive road-wheels on sprung pivot arms as well as the pivoted front road-wheels seen in the earlier Christie-based designs. It was a simple tank with a rough but serviceable finish that was ideal for mass production. It had all-round sloping armour and was armed with the 76.2mm anti-tank gun, which was a much larger calibre than most tanks used at that stage.

Thanks to Kulik's opposition to any sort of tank development, the initial model T-34 was fated to be armed with an inadequate main gun. There were three contenders: the L-11 from the Kirov factory in Leningrad, and the F-32 and the F-34 from Factory no. 92 at Gorkiy (formerly Nizhny Novgorod). Although the latter was the superior weapon and was ready for production, Kulik ensured that his Kirov factory got the work. Vasiliy Grabin, head of the design bureau at Gorkiy, took matters into his own hands and ordered the creation of a reserve stock of F-34s.

Kulik's failure to authorise full production of the F-34 meant that the T-34 Model 1940 was armed with the L-11 and the KV-1 Model 1940 with the F-32. All subsequent models of both tanks were armed with the superior F-34, much to Kulik's fury. The F-34 gun stayed in service until it was replaced by the D-5T and ZiS-S-53 85mm guns in the T-34/85. Kulik's ineptitude also resulted in a shortage of 76.2mm shells, which meant that many T-34s and KV-1s went into battle without their full complement of ammunition.

The T-34 tank weighed in at just over 26 tons and its V-2-34 500hp diesel engine, located in the rear of the hull, gave it a top road speed of 30mph and a range of 302km, though with additional fuel tanks this could be extended to 450km. The diesel engine already in use in the BT-7M not only greatly increased the operational range but also reduced the risk of fire. The development and manufacture of the diesel engine was kept secret even from Stalin's inner circle. Nikita Khrushchev, First Secretary of the Ukrainian Central Committee, was deliberately kept in the dark, 'Stalin told me that diesel engines were being manufactured at the Kharkov locomotive factory. Naturally I knew of this factory, but this was the first I'd heard about diesels being made there. . . . they did prove very effective when used to power our T-34 tanks.'

German Armaments
Minister Albert Speer
examining a captured
Model 1940 T-34.

   Notably, the tracks were almost 2ft wide; this greatly helped to spread the weight of the tank, allowing it to travel over mud and snow with ease. The track design was also unusual in that the wide track plates were held together by simple steel pins retained by buffers attached to the hull; when in motion, these buffers pushed back into place any projecting pin heads as they passed by. This greatly simplified track manufacture as well as maintenance in the field. The hull fighting compartment was divided internally by a bulkhead separating the engine from the four-man crew. The driver sat at the front with the co-driver, who operated a machine gun mounted in the hull glacis plate; the commander/gunner and loader manned the turret.

   On 19 December 1939, despite the prototype being incomplete, the Soviet high command accepted the T-34 for adoption by the Red Army's tank and mechanised units. In early February 1940 two tanks under the personal direction of Koshkin were tested on a trial run from Kharkov via Moscow, Smolensk, Kiev and back to Kharkov. Koshkin could have delegated this task to members of his design team, but he was determined to prove the superiority of his A-32 concept over the A-30. It was a decision that was to cost him dearly.

This photograph highlights the hazards presented by the T-34's single hatch. German panzer commanders liked to fight with their heads out of the turret for a 360° view of the battlefield, hence the development of the raised cupola. The T-34 commander, who was also responsible for firing the gun, had to either expose himself to the side of the hatch or sit on the turret roof.

In Moscow the T-34 was presented to Stalin and the high command as something radically different from previous Soviet tanks. Although dubbed the T-34, the first tanks were not ready until March 1940. The design was given the green light for mass production in June 1940 once the manufacturing drawings were completed.

The clouds of war gathering across Europe meant Koshkin's creation was rushed into production and in consequence suffered many mechanical defects. Nonetheless the T-34 was the very first real tank in the modern sense – Koshkin had achieved an almost perfect balance between firepower, mobility and armour protection. No one had ever really managed it up until this point, and no tank designer could really match the combination during the course of the Second World War. Koshkin had produced a tank that was well suited to armoured combat and could cope easily with the unforgiving Russian landscape and weather.

This T-34 Model 1941/42 gives some idea of the size of the single hatch. When open, it also exposed the loader. It was only with the Model 1943 that separate hatches were introduced for the commander and loader, and even then only the final models were fitted with a 360° commander's cupola. The main armament is mounted noticeably higher than on the Model 1941.

Germans troops examining the distinctive cast mantle of a Model 1943.

(*Opposite, top*) This burnt-out Model 1942 is recognisable by its cast (as opposed to rolled plate) turret. Note the twin periscopes for the commander and loader; these were introduced on the Model 1941, but wartime shortages often meant the loader's periscope was omitted.

(*Opposite, below*) Another burnt-out T-34. This is a Model 1943 T-34/76D with the cast hexagonal turret, twin hatches and lighter spoked wheels. This turret was originally designed for the proposed T-34M, which was designed to have torsion bar suspension as used on the KV and T-50 tanks.

The turret grab rails just visible on this Model 1943 were designed for tank *desants* (tank riding infantry). This was a battlefield necessity due to the Red Army's lack of armoured personnel carriers.

Whatever credit General Pavlov might take for the T-34, Khrushchev had very little time for Pavlov's abilities: 'I remember in 1940 watching him, when he was commander of our armoured tank forces, test our new T-34 tanks in Kharkov. On the basis of a short conversation with him, I decided he was a man of very limited scope.' Unfortunately for Khruschev (and, indeed, the Soviet Union), Stalin was not receptive to his reservations. On the eve of war, in the light of his expertise in armoured warfare, Pavlov was appointed commander of the vital Western Military District.

General Georgi Zhukov noted, 'The new tanks began appearing in the tank schools and in the border military districts only in the later half of 1940.' Sadly, Koshkin never got to evaluate his creation in combat, nor to upgrade it. During the trials he contracted pneumonia and died in hospital on 26 September 1940.

The first 1940 production model had a rolled plate turret and was armed with the short L-11 or L/30.5 Model 1938 tank gun. This was carried in a very distinctive bulbous cast and contoured cradle, which was welded to an external mantlet above the barrel. The first 115 tanks to roll off the factory floor were also fitted with a ball-mounted machine gun in the rear of the turret, but this feature was subsequently

The following photographs illustrate the T-34's suspension from rear to front. The rear drive sprocket is larger than the front idler, and there is a characteristic gap between the first two wheels and the remaining three.

The rubber-rimmed, spoke road-wheel. These were solid discs on the early models, but the spoke and hole design was intended to make the wheel lighter and stronger. The double wheel rim visible on the right shows where the track links engaged with the main wheels.

The rear drive sprocket is larger than the front as the transmission and drive train are in the rear.

A close-up of the front idler.

The T-34's metal track links. The protruding track pins are clearly visible and are relatively easy to remove should the tracks need repairing. As the tracks pass the front of the hull the pin heads are pushed back in by a buffer. Initially the poor-quality steel used for the pins meant they had a tendency to snap as the tank made a turn. Use of all-metal wheels resulted in considerable vibration through the metal track links. Under combat conditions the crews tended to use a mix of rubber and metal rim wheels.

The hull front, showing the armoured mount of the hull machine gun, the driver's hatch and spare track links secured to the front. The T-34 carried a 7.62mm Degtaryev DT machine gun in the hull and the turret.

discarded. The T-34 had 45mm of frontal armour and 40mm on the sides. On the early models the large disc wheels had the luxury of solid rubber tyres, but as the war progressed, resulting in ever-increasing shortages of raw materials, steel-rimmed wheels were adopted instead.

The first T-34 turret was constructed from rolled plate welded together, but in order to accelerate production Koshkin's former assistant Alexander Morozov designed a new turret that could be cast. Also in mid-1941 the newer tank gun with a longer barrel was installed. More improvements followed and the following year a new T-34 model was produced with a hexagonal turret that lent itself to even greater mass production. Also to help speed up hull manufacture Yevgeny Paton introduced a new system of automatic welding on the production lines. In addition, the fuel tank capacity was increased and the hull equipped with exterior fuel tanks that further increased the operational range.

The Germans first came across the initial production model in the summer of 1941 and dubbed it the T-34/76A; this name stuck, although the Soviets did not bother with such categorisation. Soviet troops simply called it the *Prinadlezhit-*

*Chetverki* ('Thirty-Four'). The German name was also adopted by the British and has remained in general usage ever since.

The second production model, dubbed the T-34/76B, came out in 1941 and had the longer and more powerful F-34 Model 1940 L/41.5 76.2mm gun. Notably, the vast gun cradle was replaced by a fabricated bolted assembly, which was easier to produce. Later versions of this type had twin horn periscopes for the commander and loader instead of the single one previously fitted. The 1942 production programme also included a B version with a cast turret instead of the previous welded type. Some of these were converted to the flamethrower role under the designation ATO-41. Towards the end of 1942 the chassis was used to build some of the Red Army's very first self-propelled guns in the shape of the SU-122 (see Chapter 3). Mass production of these commenced in December 1942. During the winter of 1942/3 the tank also gained a commander's cupola on top of the turret. A five-speed gear box was also introduced, along with a new clutch.

Essentially there were five main production runs of the T-34. The first was the Model 1940 (T-34/76A), of which about 400 were built with the L-11 76.2mm tank gun. This was followed by the Model 1941 (T-34/76B) with thicker armour and the superior F-34 gun. The Model 1942 (T-34/76C) also had thicker armour and a number of manufacturing improvements. Confusingly the Model 1943 (with three variants dubbed the T-34/76D, E, and F) was actually first introduced from May 1942. Most notably, it had the new hexagonal turret (nicknamed 'Mickey Mouse' by the Germans because the twin turret-roof hatches, when opened, resembled that character's rounded ears). This turret did away with the rear overhang of the earlier models, which acted as a shell trap and were a tempting target for German Teller anti-tank mines. The new turret was also slightly larger, offering the crew extra space. Later production versions also featured a new commander's cupola.

Following the German invasion, the T-34 was swiftly forced from its birthplace. Fortunately for the Red Army, the Kharkov Locomotive Factory had begun evacuating to Nizhny Tagil in August 1941. Leningrad's Kirov tank plant was moved to join with the existing Chelyabinsk tractor works. This enormous tank-building complex became known, appropriately enough, as Tankograd or 'Tank city'. In addition, other plants were set up; Krasnoye Sormovo at Gorkiy near Moscow produced tanks with the new cast turret, while the STZ plant near Stalingrad produced the welded turrets. In the autumn of 1942 tank production at Stalingrad was closed down due to the heavy fighting in the city. Instead production was extended at Tankograd and the Ural Heavy Machine Tool Factory in Sverdlovsk was converted to produce T-34s. The need to upgun the T-34 led to these factories shifting production over to the T-34/85 from 1943 onwards.

# Chapter Two

# A Winning Upgrade –
# T-34/85

To counter the German Tiger tank, which first appeared on the Russian front in 1943, the Soviets adapted their 85mm Model 1939 anti-aircraft gun for anti-tank use. Once modified, it had an effective range of 1,000m (1,100 yards) and could penetrate 100mm of armour, so it constituted a very real threat to the German Panther and Tiger tanks, although it was far from accurate at long range. Towards the end of the summer of 1943 the gun was installed into a heavy cast turret and fitted to the redundant KV-1 chassis, which became the KV-85. This was produced as a stopgap until the heavy IS tank was ready. Limited numbers of the IS-1 armed with an 85mm gun appeared in late 1943 and were issued to the Red Army, followed by the improved IS-2 upgunned with a 122mm weapon in early 1944.

In 1943 a small number of up-armoured T-34s were manufactured with much thicker armour. Designated T-43s, they sported 110mm frontal armour and 75mm on the sides, a new five-speed gearbox and the late pattern turret. They were, however, still armed with the 76.2mm gun, which was inadequate in the face of the new German 75mm and 88mm high-velocity tank and anti-tank guns, which were appearing in ever-greater numbers. Ultimately the T-43 was not very successful as the increased weight greatly reduced the tank's performance and it was swiftly superseded by the KV-85 and T-34/85.

During the summer of 1943 Alexander Morozov, who had taken over from the late Mikhail Koshkin as chief designer, redesigned the T-34 to take a new turret armed with an 85mm gun on a par with the KV-85 and SU-85. Adapting the cast turret designed for the KV-85, he introduced standardisation between the two classes of tank. Later the turret was redesigned and a second model of the T-34/85 was produced. The Model 1943 turret displayed a unique style of bolted collar and was armed with the shorter D-5T 85mm gun, which was capable of penetrating the frontal armour of the German Tiger at 1,000 metres, although accuracy remained a problem. This interim model also featured a rounded front-hull join, rounded front fenders and no turret fillet.

The T-34/85's larger turret allowed for a five-man crew instead of four. This freed up the commander, who had previously fired the main gun as well as directing the tank. Also the frontal armour was increased to a maximum of 75mm. Despite the numerous improvements and refinements that had been introduced since 1940, the T-34 remained a simple and rugged design that was well suited to mass production. The basic T-34 chassis still included the V-2 diesel engine of 500hp driving the rear sprockets and the Christie-style suspension of large road-wheels on pivot arms controlled by long coil springs.

The larger-calibre armament provided greater ballistic range and combat parity with the German heavy tanks; this, combined with ever-growing numbers, was a war-winning combination. The T-34/85 was approved for mass production on 15 December 1943. By the end of the year 283 had been produced and during the following year a further 11,000 were built. Approximately 800 examples of the T-34/85 Model 1943 were produced at Gorkiy early in 1944.

The T-34/85 had three distinctive wartime production models. The Model 1943 had a short production run with the D-5T 85mm gun. This was followed by the Model 1944, which was produced from March 1944 through to the end of that year; it featured the simpler ZiS-S-53 85mm gun and a new gunner's sight. The internal layout was improved and the radio moved from the hull into the turret. Finally the Model 1945 was, somewhat confusingly, manufactured from 1944 to 1945, with an electrically powered turret traverse motor, an enlarged commander's cupola with a one-piece hatch, and the TDP (*tankovoy dimoviy pribor*) smoke system with electrically detonated MDSh canisters. This remained in production until the mid-1950s, when the T-54 tank was adopted. After the war there was a Model 1946, plus there were refurbishment programmes in 1960 and in 1969.

The T-34/85 Model 1945 differed from the Model 1944 in that it featured a larger cupola, which extended close to the port edge of the turret, requiring a tiny lip underneath on the turret side. Although the Red Army did not differentiate between the variants, the Model 1946 entered service during early 1945 and saw front-line action in the closing days of the 'Great Patriotic War'. It could be distinguished from the Model 1945 by its fuller lower turret sides and the new configuration of ventilator domes. Another improved variant developed that year was known as the T-44, but it did not see service until the early post-war years.

Nikolai Yakovlevic Zheleznov served with the 63rd Brigade, 4th Tank Army. He recalled:

In essence, until we got the 85mm gun we had to run from Tigers like rabbits, and look for an opportunity to turn back and get at their flanks. It was difficult. If you saw a Tiger 800–1,000 metres away and it started 'crossing' you, while

The enlarged turret of the T-34/85 allowed for an 85mm main gun and provided space for three crewmen, freeing up the commander, who had previously acted as commander/main gunner. This 36th Guards Tank Brigade tank was photographed in Belgrade in 1944. It is either the Model 1943 or the subsequent Model 1944. The man at the back is leaning on the twin ventilator domes.

The Model 1945 T-34/85 featured a larger commander's cupola than its predecessor and had a forward-opening three-quarter hatch. Also visible are the two separated armoured ventilator fan domes.

In many ways the T-34/76 was just a stopgap until 1943; it was the advent of the T-34/85 that really gave the Red Army a war-winner.

it moved its gun horizontally you could stay in your tank, but once it started moving it vertically you'd better jump out, or you could get burned! It never happened to me, but other guys baled out. But when the T-34/85 entered service, we could stand up against enemy tanks one on one.

On 12 August 1944 the massive Tiger II went into combat for the first time on the Eastern Front with Schwere Panzer Abteilung 501 in the fighting against the Soviets' Baranów bridgehead. In this action Guards Lieutenant Os'kin's T-34/85, from the 53rd Guards Tank Brigade, knocked out three Tiger IIs by hitting their side armour from an ambush position.

### T-34 Engine
The Kharkov V-2-34 engine is mounted in the back of the T-34's hull with the transmission to the rear and cooling radiators on either side. The V-type four-stroke twelve-cylinder water-cooled diesel engine, developed for the BT-7M fast tank, generates 493bhp, which translates into a power-to-weight ratio of 17.9bhp per ton.

Depending on the conditions, the engine gives the T-34 a road speed of 34mph (54km/h) and cross-country anything from between 10mph and 15.6mph (16km/h and 25km/h) with a fuel consumption of 0.65 gallons per mile (1.84 litres/km).

The top of the engine can be accessed from an armoured inspection hatch in the middle of the rear hull deck. Turret overhang means that on both the T-34/76 and the T-34/85 the turret has to be side-on in order for the hatch to be raised. The engine can also be accessed from the inside via an inspection plate at the back of the fighting compartment, along with the batteries located on either side of the engine.

In the T-34/76 a Cyclone air filter sits on top of the V-2 and there are warm air extraction vents over the transmission; the initial Pomon air filter proved wholly inadequate and greatly restricted the engine's operating capacity. In later models two Cyclone air cleaners were installed under the rear of the engine deck. There are also warm air vents over the radiators on the sides of the hull. This air extraction made the rear deck of the T-34, despite the fumes, a warm place for Red Army 'tank riders' to crouch on when hitching a ride in cold weather.

Under the air extraction vents, the transmission, braking assembly, exhausts and air filter pipes are protected by two steel shutters that can be opened vertically or shut horizontally. In the closed position they help heat the engine on start up and protect the area from shell splinters during combat; however, the engine can overheat if they are left down too long.

As the transmission is in the rear, it means that the driving and fighting compartments are not obstructed by a drive train running from the engine to the front of the tank, as in the American M3 and M4 series tanks. (The latter have a rear-mounted engine with front transmission and drive sprockets.) As a result the T-34's rear drive sprocket is much larger than the front idler, which tensions the track. The Soviets never managed to match the German Maybach transmission used in their panzers and the T-34's transmission was problematic during much of the war. Reportedly T-34 crews sometimes carried a spare strapped on the engine deck.

This was in part due to poor quality control on the production lines in terms of both raw materials and manufacturing standards. At the start of the war the rapid expansion of tank production inevitably meant that sub-component manufacture could not keep pace. A shortage of the new V-2 engines resulted in some of the early T-34s being equipped with the older Mikulin M-17T gasoline engine (ironically, a licensed copy of the German BMW VI V-12 liquid-cooled aircraft piston engine) as used in the BT-7, T-28 and T-35 tanks. Such shortages meant that the initial T-34s built at Gorkiy ended up with substandard aero engines and transmissions.

The engine layout of the T-34 – and therefore maintenance – was far simpler than in its German counterparts. The panzers were designed as front wheel drive with the Maybach V-12 engine in the rear and the gearbox in the front. Power from the

(*Above and opposite*) This is a late war production model – built in April 1945, it is either a Model 1945 or Model 1946 T-34/85. This tank served with the Red Army and the Czech Army; it was refurbished for the Egyptians, but when the deal fell through it went into the Czech reserves.

engine was transmitted from the flywheel end of the crankshaft by a propeller shaft running under the floor of the fighting compartment. Drive to the front sprockets was by shafts from the gearbox to Wilson-type epicyclic track/brake steering units operated by levers. Hatches in the front glacis plate allowed access to the gearbox and differential assembly. As with all panzers, track tension was adjusted at the rear idler wheel.

In the case of the Panther, the engine and clutch were in the rear with a propeller shaft running to the gearbox and brake/steering transmission unit in the front. In the centre of the hull was a hydraulic power take-off for the turret and main gun. Likewise with the Tiger I, power was taken from the engine forward via a transmission driveshaft under the fighting compartment floor to the gearbox located to the right of the driver. The Tiger II had a similar set-up with an engine compartment the same as that of the Panther.*

Over the years the Soviet V-2 engine was variously upgraded and was also installed in many of the Red Army's heavy tanks. The initial 1937 production model was used in the BT-7M while the follow-on V-2-34 was installed in the T-34, SU-85 and SU-100. The V-2K was used in the KV-1 and KV-2 while the V-2-10 powered the ISU self-propelled guns and the Joseph Stalin tanks. These variants generated 450–850hp.

Just as the very first Kharkov V-2 diesel engine went into production Stalin had its designer shot. The man responsible for the early work on the V-2 was Konstantin Fyodorovich Chelpan, head of the Engineering Design Bureau at the Kharkov Locomotive Factory. His team's key innovations included producing an engine from a lightweight aluminium alloy, and they were the first to install a diesel engine in a tank. Crucially, it was the shortage of aluminium that thwarted the Germans' attempts to copy the V-2 and the T-34.

Chelpan did not live to see the V-2-34 or the T-34. He was arrested in late 1937 accused of being a foreign saboteur and a spy, thanks to his mixed Ukrainian/Greek heritage. The fact that he had been educated in the late 1920s in Germany, Switzerland and the UK only exacerbated his vulnerable political position. Under torture he confessed and the following year was executed. Stalin's security apparatus claimed that Chelpan had died of congestive heart failure. He was not politically rehabilitated until the mid-1950s and Chelpan's true cause of death was only officially acknowledged in 1988.

---

* See the author's Images of War Special. Tiger I & Tiger II.

| V-2 Variants | Use |
| --- | --- |
| V-2 | 1937 production model, powered the BT-7M. |
| V-2-34 | 500hp, 1939 model revised hull mounts, fuel and cooling connectors and refined clutch. Powered the T-34, SU-85 and SU-100. |
| V-2K | 600hp, 1939 model increased injection pressure and higher engine speed. Powered the KV-1 and KV-2. |
| V-2V | 375hp, 1940 model detuned for use in lighter vehicles. Powered the Voroshilovets artillery tractor. |
| V-2L/P | Maritime version not put into production. |
| V-2SN | 862hp, 1940 model with a supercharger from the Mikulin AM-38 aircraft engine. Powered the KV-3. |
| V-2-10 (V-2IS) | 520hp, 1943 model stronger cylinders and heads, improved fuel pump, larger radiator and oil cooler and modified hull mounts. Powered the IS-2, ISU-122 and ISU-152, and the T-10. |
| V-2-450AV-S3 | 450hp, modified for use in the oil drilling industry. |

The T-34 driver's position. Visible are the manual clutch pedal and foot brake, the steering levers on either side of the seat and the two compressed air bottles used to start the diesel engine in cold weather. Driving is hard work, with the controls demanding a lot of physical effort.

The co-axial DT machine gun in the T-34/85 turret.

The T-34/85 turret interior. From left to right: the telescopic gunsight, the 85mm gun breech and the co-axial machine gun.

## T-34 Starting and Driving Procedure

To start the engine, the driver has to switch on the battery master switch, select a fuel tank for fuel and make sure the gear lever is in neutral. There is provision for priming the fuel system by pressurising the selected fuel tank with a hand-operated air pump (directly in front of the driver's feet), then using a tap by the driver's left shoulder to vent off any air in the fuel.

The driver then has to press the oil pump switch to prime the engine lubrication system, preventing the engine starting up 'dry', with resulting excessive wear. On depressing the foot throttle and pressing the starter button, the engine should start immediately, then the hand throttle is set for a fast tick-over. The driver then checks the oil pressure and ensures that the dynamo is charging.

In extreme cold, or with a discharged battery, there is an emergency air-starting system for the engine, using two compressed air cylinders in front of the driver's feet. To operate this the driver has to open the valves on the air cylinders, then, using the same procedure as above, open the air-start control valve. As soon as the engine starts, all the valves must be closed, as the cylinders have to be removed for refilling.

The T-34 has the conventional clutch, brake and throttle pedal layout. Steering is controlled by pulling the two tillers or levers on either side of the driver's seat, left to turn left, right to turn right. Pulling a tiller halfway back disconnects the steering clutch on that side, taking power off that track. The harder the vehicle is working, the sharper the turn. To increase the turn, the driver simply pulls the tiller hard back; this applies the track brake. Pull hard enough and it will stop that track altogether, causing a sharp slew turn.

If both tillers are pulled halfway back, all drive to the tracks is disconnected; pulling both tillers hard back will stop the vehicle – all without touching the foot clutch or brake pedals. Using these steering clutches to feed in drive just to one or other track can be very useful when manoeuvring in confined spaces.

The driver needs to steer in a series of hard pulls; continuously pulling gently on a steering brake will burn it out. When going down a steep slope, and relying on engine braking, the driver has to remember that disengaging, say, the right steering clutch, without pulling hard back for the steering brake, will make the vehicle swing to the left, as there will no longer be any braking on the right track. When travelling at speed on some surfaces it is possible to lock one track, and the tank will continue almost straight ahead, with the track just skidding.

Gear selection and changing is classic crash gearbox practice, with double declutching needed for each gear change. Pull away as with any vehicle, build up speed in the low gear, clutch down, and lift off throttle, gear lever into neutral, set engine revs for the next gear, clutch up and spin the gearbox, clutch down, select next gear and clutch up. When changing from first to second gear, especially on soft

At the rear of the T-34/85 turret are ammunition storage racks. Further rounds are located in bins in the hull floor. These bins are covered by neoprene matting that folds back.

Ammunition racks holding spare drums for the turret machine gun.

A sleeping space for one. This bedding mat has been rolled out over the hull floor, beneath which are spare 85mm rounds.

ground, the tank will probably stop before the driver can engage second! When changing down, the engine revs must be increased to exactly the revs needed for the lower gear. Whether changing up or down, getting the engine revs right is critical — it doesn't just make a dreadful noise, but the gear lever will jar the driver's wrist, and he won't get it into gear. The tank then will stop, becoming a sitting target.

Old lorries used to have a latch on the gear lever, which you lifted to engage reverse. The T-34 has just such a latch, but it has to be held for every gear except reverse and crawler. There is no handbrake as such, but there is a pawl that can be pulled to hold the footbrake down. In trained hands the T-34 was quite agile and could run rings round the panzers; in untrained hands it was a completely different matter.

## Colour Schemes and Camouflage

On the whole the Red Army was not very imaginative with the paint schemes applied to the T-34. The photographic evidence is fairly slim, and black and white images do not help greatly — especially with photographs of knocked-out tanks, where it is not easy to decide if any visible mottling is camouflage paint, scorch marks, or simply dirt and dust. Those colour photographs that are readily available show T-34/76s painted a dark green, and often caked in a layer of very fine dust. Summer on the Russian steppe was a dusty time and tank crews sometimes concealed their tanks with straw. The net effect of all this was to make it appear that the tank was a soft olive green.

Generally, T-34s were finished in factory dark green, subsequently adorned by the crews with unit markings and propaganda slogans. As the war on the Eastern Front progressed during the summer months a few attempts were made to camouflage the T-34s with three-tone or two-tone schemes. These comprised dark green, brown and sand or just dark green and sand. Certainly at Kursk some T-34/76 Model 1943 tanks sported a dark green and khaki camouflage. Once the Red Army went firmly over to the counterattack they saw little reason to camouflage their tanks — in contrast the outnumbered panzers had to do everything they could to conceal themselves from the T-34s.

Essentially, during the winter the Russian landscape meant tanks operated either in the flat open white steppe, with its almost complete absence of colour, or in the confines of forests, woods, brush and villages, where there was a variety of greys and browns. The open country simply required white paint to help conceal the tank, but the complicated outlines of forests and settlements needed a two-colour disruptive winter paint scheme that would blur the tank's outline.

In the winter months the T-34 was overpainted with whitewash that sometimes encompassed the whole tank but very often did not extend to the road-wheels. The T-34/76s encountered by the Wehrmacht at Mtensk in October 1941 had

This photograph shows the crude finish on the turret casting. There was no time for finesse in the Soviet tank factories.

whitewash crudely applied over their factory base colour, but this does not seem to have extended over the suspension or the rear of the hull. A lot depended on how close the crews were to the front when it came to whitewashing their tanks. The finish also depended on whether they hand-painted with brushes, brooms or rags or employed a compressor spray gun. Brush strokes tended to leave the tank streaky, while spraying could produce a mottling effect. Inevitably the whitewash did not stay white very long and quickly became streaked with mud and rust, giving the tank a dirty orange colour. The whitewash also tended to wear off fairly quickly. Some T-34/76s were given a winter grey and white two-tone camouflage.

According to Soviet winter camouflage guidelines, painting in two colours with large spots could be achieved in two ways. The first, and easiest, involved painting only part of the tank white, leaving a quarter or a third of its surface green; the other method was more time-consuming and meant repainting the entire tank in either white and dark grey or white and grey-brown. The winter two-tone schemes did not

It was common practice to store spare track links in the turret hand rails. This was not so much to provide easy access to the links but rather to offer a crude level of up-armouring.

Crews in a column of T-34/85s making the most of a lull in the fighting.

want any degree of uniformity – far from it. Often within a platoon a number of tanks would be all white, while others would have irregular stripes with some of the green still showing; others might have white with dark grey spots or white with white and greyish brown spots. Some T-34s were given a lattice pattern effect on their turrets and hulls to break up their outlines.

As well as painting their tanks for winter combat, the T-34 crews were warned about covering up tank tracks in the snow as these were clearly visible from the air and from nearby high ground. This was especially so with the T-34's very wide tracks. In a way operating in powdery snow was a bit like operating in the desert, but instead of throwing up sand when travelling at speed, the T-34 could give itself away thanks to the clouds of powdery snow. As a result, during the winter tank crews were required to move at low speeds, especially in fresh snow.

Likewise the crews were warned that anything over 3 inches of snow reduced the tank's speed – bearing in mind that the T-34 could easily cope with snow up to 3ft deep, this meant that the element of surprise could easily be lost on the approach to the point of combat. Deep snow forced the T-34s to use existing roads, but on the dark strips of churned-up roads the all-white winter paint would stand out to any reconnaissance aircraft, and therefore tank commanders were instructed to travel on the side of the road closest to the sun so that their tank's shadow fell on the road. Tank tracks stood out on white snow, but could be obliterated by sweeping a road. Similarly, graders could remove tracks left on a hard frozen crush.

The T-34/85 was mainly either dark green or whitewashed depending on the time of year. During the 1944–45 operations Soviet heavy tanks often sported a horizontal white recognition band around the upper part of the turret; this practice also extended to the T-34/85. The combat air recognition flag of the Red Army consisted of a yellow star outline on a red background and was carried on the rear decking of the tank.

# Chapter Three

# T-34 Variants

Nearly a dozen roles were found for the robust T-34 chassis, principally as self-propelled guns and tank destroyers. Following the German invasion, the Soviets sought to outgun German armour; the challenge for the designers was to marry the gun to the mount, which was easier said than done. The Red Army had been particularly impressed by the German *Sturmgeschütz* assault gun and sought to emulate it.

Once the Soviets had phased out most of their light and medium tanks, only the T-34 and KV chassis remained in production to provide an upgunned platform. By the autumn of 1942 the Red Army was encountering the German Tiger tank, the armour of which was too thick to be penetrated by the 76.2mm guns of the T-34 and KV-1 from a safe range. The following summer they also had to contend with the Panther. Now more than ever the Red Army needed a more powerful main armament.

### T-34/57 Tank Hunter

As a stopgap measure, in 1941 and 1943 some T-34s were fitted out for use as tank hunters with a ZiS-2, ZiS-4 or ZiS-4M high-velocity 57mm gun. This weapon actually had better penetration than the F-34 76.2mm but its small bore meant its high explosive shell was too small to be used against unarmoured targets. Around 324 T-34s are believed to have been converted to this role.

### SU-122 Self-Propelled Gun

The SU-122 was the first of several self-propelled guns based on the T-34 to be put into series production. SU stands for *Samokhodnaya Ustanovka*, meaning 'self-propelled carriage'. It was created by removing the T-34's turret and installing a Model 1938 122mm field howitzer in the hull using a limited traverse mount at the front of the vehicle. A simple box superstructure was created that followed the existing slope of the tank's front armour. The gun was held in a enormous mantlet with a fabricated armoured cover for the very prominent recoil system.

Doing away with the turret allowed for a larger fighting compartment to house the gun breech and made it cheaper and easier to manufacture than a regular tank. However, aiming the gun required manoeuvring the entire vehicle. This rather cumbersome-looking vehicle was designed in 1942, with the first production vehicles coming into service in January 1943, initially as the SU-35. This was the culmination of work carried out on the SG-122 based on the German StuG III and the U-34 (armed with the standard 76.2mm tank gun), neither of which went into production. Crucially, the SU-122 lacked a hull machine gun.

Late 1942 saw the formation of the first self-propelled regiments equipped with the SU-122. They consisted of two batteries of SU-122s with some eight vehicles, and four batteries of lighter SU-76 assault guns with a total of seventeen vehicles. The SU-122 was deployed in platoons of three providing close fire support for the tank divisions. They were first used to equip the 1433rd and 1434th Self-Propelled Artillery Regiments. These joined the 54th Army on the Volkhov Front near Leningrad, which had been commanded by General Kulik, the former head of the artillery directive, until he was court-martialled for incompetence in March 1942.

The combination of the SU-76 and the SU-122 was not ideal, especially as the former had an open fighting compartment. As a result, the SU-122s were organised into separate units. The massive gun proved effective with direct fire against enemy strongholds, while the concussion from its high explosive rounds could blast the turret off a Tiger tank at close range. The SU-122 was phased out in late 1943 and replaced by the SU-152, based on the robust KV chassis. However, production continued into the summer of 1944, by which time around 1,150 had been completed.

## SU-85 Tank Destroyer

In order to develop a tank that was roughly equivalent to the Tiger, during the summer of 1943 the Soviets worked to upgrade the KV-1 by fitting a new turret armed with an 85mm gun. Similarly, a tank destroyer or tank hunter variant of the T-34 was supplied to the Red Army in August 1943 by fitting the D-5T high-velocity 85mm anti-tank gun into the limited traverse mount of the SU-122 superstructure. This vehicle presented a low profile to enemy tanks and enjoyed the mobility of the T-34, but the trade-off with the hull-mounted gun, as with the SU-122, was relatively thin armour.

Around 100 had been built by the end of 1943 and the following year production was continued to replace the SU-76 self-propelled gun, which was relegated to an infantry support role. Two versions appeared: the basic type, which had a fixed commander's cupola with a rotating periscope and three vision blocks, and the SU-85M, which had the same casemate as the follow-on SU-100 and the T-34/85 commander's cupola.

The SU-122 self-propelled gun married a 122mm howitzer with the T-34 chassis. It was not very successful, with just over a thousand being built.

The SU-85 was designed to stand off and destroy enemy armoured vehicles and bunkers. As a result, it also lacked a self-defence machine gun and, like the German Ferdinand/Elefant, was very vulnerable to enemy infantry at close quarters. The SU-85 first saw combat along the Dnepr river in August 1943 and was initially popular as it was one of the few tanks that could take on the Tiger and the Panther.

The SU-85s were issued to two types of self-propelled unit: battalions, equipped with twelve SU-85s, which were assigned to Army and Corps level and the larger regiments, each with four batteries of sixteen SU-85s in total. The SU-85 was swiftly superseded by the T-34/85 so production was halted in late 1944 when 2,050 had been built. The production lines were instead switched to the SU-100 and the remaining SU-85s were withdrawn after the war ended.

### SU-100 Tank Destroyer

As the SU-85 offered no advantages over the T-34/85, it was decided to develop an upgunned version. The SU-100 appeared in September 1944 and was essentially the same vehicle as the SU-85 but armed with a 100mm Model 1944 high-velocity gun fitted in a larger mantlet. This made it one of the best self-propelled anti-tank guns of the war as it could cut through 125mm of vertical armour up to 2,000 metres and could penetrate the German Panther tank's sloped 85mm frontal armour at a range of 1,500 metres. Its hull also boasted major improvements over its predecessor, with the frontal armour increased from 45mm to 75mm and a new commander's area provided by a sponson on the right side of the hull; this, combined with the commander's cupola, allowed him to be more effective in directing his crew.

The only real drawback with this vehicle was the length of the gun barrel, which greatly reduced manoeuvrability. As a result, it was not suited to fighting in forests or

The M-30 Model 1938 122mm howitzer was used to create the SU-122.

(*Above, right*) In order to house the 122mm, the T-34 hull was fitted with a raised armoured casemate with 45mm frontal armour. This allowed for a five-man crew.

Close-up of the 122mm breech. It was designed as a howitzer and the low muzzle velocity meant it made a poor anti-tank weapon. Introduction of the BP-460A High Explosive Anti-Tank (HEAT) round did little to alleviate the problem.`

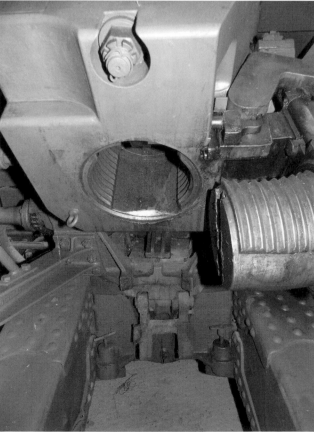

urban warfare. No doubt it would have struggled on some country roads, particularly in the Carpathian Mountains, where negotiating hairpin bends would have been completely out of the question. This tank destroyer saw widespread service during 1945 and was used to help defeat Hitler's ill-fated spring offensive in Hungary. By July that year Soviet tank factories had produced 2,335 SU-100s. It was much more successful than its predecessor and remained in service well into the late 1950s.

### TT-34 Armoured Recovery Vehicle
Some battle-damaged T-34s were converted to the T-34T or TT-34 (*tyagach* – 'tractor') armoured recovery role with the removal of the turret. The turret ring was either plated over or a superstructure added for the crew, and they were used for towing.

### SKP-5 Armoured Recovery Vehicle
The SKP-5 was the first specialised recovery vehicle. It comprised a T-34 chassis carrying a 360° traverse crane with a 5-ton capacity.

### T-34/MTU Bridgelayer
There were at least three types of bridgelayer based on the T-34 and designated the T-34/MTU. These included an 'ARK'-type bridge fitted to the vehicle, while another was a rigid arm launched bridge (the MTU), as well as a Czech-designed folding scissor bridge; these, however, were postwar designs. The ARK featured an adjustable platform instead of the turret and the bridge could not be removed from the tank. The driver simply drove the tank into the gap that needed bridging and the bridge was then adjusted to the required height.

### T-34-T Crane
After the Second World War a number of T-34s were fitted with specialised engineering equipment. The early 1950s saw the introduction of the T-34-T, which included a rigging assembly, loading platform and jib crane. The rear deck was reinforced so that the cargo platform had a weight capability of 2.5 tons.

### T-34/STU Dozer
Some T-34s were fitted with 'dozer blades and were designated the T-34/STU.

### OT-34 Flamethrower
The OT-34 and OT-34-85 flamethrower tanks had an internally mounted ATO-41 (Model 1941) or ATO-42 (Model 1942) flamethrower with the nozzle replacing the

The SU-85 tank destroyer mounting an 85mm anti-tank gun was a much better proposition, but it was made redundant by the T-34/85 and was superseded by the much more powerful SU-100.

The Germans were highly impressed by the T-34 family of armoured fighting vehicles and were not averse to redeploying them, as these photographs of a captured T-34/76D and SU-85 testify.

The SU-85 provided a useful stopgap for the Red Army and by the end of 1944 over two thousand had been built.

hull machine gun. The fuel for the flamethrower was carried in an armoured tank on the back of the vehicle.

The OT-34 equipped with the ATO-42 carried 44 gallons (200 litres) of fuel and was powered by compressed air. It had a range of up to 98 yards with unthickened fuel or 120 yards with thickened fuel. The ATO-42 was operated by an electrical pump that was started by a 20mm cartridge. The OT-34 was capable of six bursts, each of about two seconds' duration.

The flamethrowers were organised into battalions consisting of one company of eleven OT-34 medium flamethrowers and two companies of KV-8 heavy flamethrowers with ten tanks. As the heavy KV-8s were lost, the flamethrower battalions were reorganised in 1943 into two companies of OT-34s supported by a company of standard T-34 gun tanks.

### PT-34 Mineclearer
For mineclearing operations there were roller-equipped variants of both the T-34/76 and the T-34/85; all were dubbed PT-34s. The rollers were propelled on arms in front

The SU-100 appeared in September 1944. This was an upgunned SU-85 with a 100mm anti-tank gun and greatly increased armour.

The SU-100 played a role in helping to crush Hitler's spring counteroffensive launched in Hungary in 1945.

This image gives a clear indication of the main drawback with the SU-100: the length of its barrel. On the open plains of Hungary this was not a problem, but on tight roads or in forests and mountains it greatly limited the tank destroyer's manoeuvrability.

of the tank. A variant was also produced using chain flails similar to those used by the British Scorpion and Crab.

Finnish minefields caused the Red Army major problems during the Winter War – in fact, it lost several thousand armoured fighting vehicles to various causes. As a result P.M. Mugalev at the Dormashina Factory in Nikolaev was instructed to design a mineclearing vehicle that could sweep a path for the assault tanks following up behind. In 1940 prototypes were tested with the cumbersome T-28 medium tank but these trials were interrupted by the German invasion and did not resume until 1942. By this time the T-28 had been thoroughly discredited by Operation Barbarossa, so the T-60 light tank and KV heavy tank chassis were tested instead. Ultimately, only the T-34, with its robust transmission and clutch, was found to be up to the job.

The plough, normally fitted to the T-34/76D, consisted of a steel fork girder frame fixed to the front of the tank. Attached at the front of the frame were two sets of steel rollers consisting of five spiked discs (each spike was actually a steel triangle with the base of the triangle facing out from the disc and pressed into the ground as the tank rolled forward to detonate mines). The drawback with this design was the gap between the two sets of rollers, which only covered the width of each track, so the tank could miss a mine and pass right over it.

The mine-roller was fitted to both the T-34/75D (seen here) and the T-34/85. The first examples saw action in the summer of 1942 and two years later helped spearhead Operation Bagration.

The OT-34 flamethrower was another T-34 variant. The fuel was carried on the back of the tank and was ejected from a nozzle in place of the hull machine gun.

While the roller fork was semi-permanently mounted on the T-34/76 or T-34/85, the rollers were normally removed when the tank was in transit. This meant that the rollers had to be installed near the front just before commencing operations. The rollers could withstand a maximum of ten detonations of up to 10kg anti-tank mines, after which they had to be replaced.

Once the design was given the green light in May 1942, trial detachments of PT-34s were created. That August two experimental PT-34s saw combat at Voronezh with the 223rd Tank Battalion, 86th Tank Brigade. Some were also used during the Battle of Stalingrad; most notably they spearheaded the assault on Kanteirovets airfield by the 16th Guards Tank Battalion during the Soviet counterattack that encircled the Germans at Stalingrad. It was not until October the following year that an initial independent engineer tank regiment with eighteen PT-34s was established, and by the end of the war there were five such regiments. The PT-34 played a leading role in Operation Bagration during the summer of 1944 and in the Vistula–Oder offensive when two regiments of mine-rollers were deployed with the advancing Red Army.

# Chapter Four

# Too Few Too Late

Panzer commander General von Mellenthin acknowledged that the Red Army 'began the war with the great advantage of possessing the T-34, a model far superior to any tank on the German side. . . . The Russian tank designers understand their job thoroughly; they cut out refinements and concentrated on the essentials – gun, power, armour and cross-country performance. During the war their system of suspension was well in advance of Germany and the West.'

On the cusp of war General Georgi Zhukov commented,

> The Defence Committee studied the situation in the tank industry on the Central Committee's direction and reported that some of the plants did not fulfil production targets, had difficulties in adjusting production processes, and that the troops were getting the KV and T-34 tanks too slowly. The Government adopted appropriate measures. The Central Committee and the Council of Peoples' Commissars passed exceptionally important decisions to organise mass production in the Volga area and in the Urals.

Zhukov appreciated that the T-34 was simply not ready in time:

> We had failed to correctly estimate the capacity of our tank industry. We required 16,600 tanks of the latest types only, and altogether as many as 32,000 tanks to equip the new mechanised corps to full strength [Stalin had authorised twenty in March 1941]. Such numbers could not be produced in a year with the existing facilities . . .
>
> We managed to equip fewer than half the corps before the war broke out. And it was those very corps that essentially repelled the first enemy blows. The corps, which at the outset of the war were still in the formative stage, were not ready until the time of the counteroffensive at Stalingrad, during which they proved decisive.

Besides Kharkov, the Soviet Union's other tank-building centre was Leningrad, where the Bolshevik, Kirov and Voroshilov factories were developing the KV heavy tank.

The fate of the Red Army's T-34s in the summer of 1941. Poor training and transmission problems meant many were simply abandoned by their inexperienced crews. The tanks in the foreground and background are Model 1940s, while the one to the left is the newer Model 1941.

(*Opposite, top*) More wrecked tanks: (from left to right) a BT-7 and two Model 1941 T-34s.

(*Opposite, below*) German officers and NCOs take a good look at an abandoned T-34/76B or Model 1941. As these men are not wearing helmets, this photograph was evidently taken well behind the German lines. Judging by the steel cable attached to the front of the hull, this was one of many T-34s that suffered mechanical failure in 1941 and was under tow before being dumped at the roadside.

This Model 1941 was hit and caught fire; the heat clearly melted the rubber rims on the wheels. The hatch is down, so it is unlikely that the crew escaped.

Progress of the latter delayed approval of the T-32 as it was Defence Commissar Marshal Kliment Voroshilov's son-in-law Zhosif Kotin who was heading the heavy tank programme. While Voroshilov dragged his feet over committing to the T-32, in August 1939 the KV-I was approved for production at the Kirov factory (although following the German siege of Leningrad the KV-I programme was shifted to Chelyabinsk). Stalin fretted that the T-32 was too complex to build, and the last thing he wanted was another T-28 medium tank or T-35 heavy tank, both of which could only be built in limited numbers. What was needed was something that could be built quickly to replace the T-26 and the BT-5/7.

Although it was intended that Kharkov would churn out 600 T-34s a month, Marshal Kulik, commander of the artillery directorate, held up deliveries of the L-II gun while Voroshilov and General Pavlov argued that the T-34 should be put on hold until a modernised version – the T-34M – was ready for mass production. This version was to have a new turret, a V-5 diesel engine and torsion bar suspension but the reality was that it would not be ready until mid-1942.

Another knocked-out Model 1941 – here the force of the blast was such that it tore the turret off or the ammunition 'cooked off', causing the turret's removal. Either way the blaze melted the rubber rims on the wheels.

Quite how these Model 1941s got into this situation is unclear; perhaps German bombers or heavy artillery caught them out in the open.

Despite the diesel engine, the T-34 still caught fire.

Thanks in part to the dithering by Stalin, Voroshilov and Pavlov, by the time of the German invasion on 22 June 1941 the Kharkov and Stalingrad tank factories had built only 1,226 T-34/76s, consisting of both the Model 1940 and the Model 1941. This meant that when Hitler's Operation Barbarossa opened, just 5 per cent of the Red Army's tank force comprised T-34s and just 2 per cent were KV-1s. The rest of the Red Army's vast tank fleet was obsolescent. Between January 1939 and 22 June 1941 the Red Army received over 7,000 new tanks, but the plants managed to put out only 1,861 KV and T-34 tanks before the war, which was clearly insufficient. The two principal tank types, the BT-7 and the T-26, were simply not up to the job by 1941.

The Western Military District facing Eastern Europe had about 982 T-34/76s and 466 KV-1s. Stalin's Baltic Military Command under Colonel General Kuznetsov was key to the defence of Leningrad and the vital Kirov tank plant. The bulk of the 1,045 tanks at Kuznetsov's disposal were old and only 105 were newer models. The 12th Mechanised Corps was able to muster 84 per cent of its tanks but the 3rd Mechanised Corps could only manage 55 per cent. The 7th Mechanised Corps had none of its authorised 420 T-34s and just forty of its 120 KVs.

General Pavlov, who had assumed command of the Western Front, had at his disposal the powerful 6th Mechanised Corps equipped with 238 T-34s; the only drawback was that they had not been issued with armour-piercing rounds and each T-34 had only a single tank of fuel. Added to that, their crews were far from proficiently trained. Within the space of a couple of weeks half the T-34s and KV-1s had been wiped out, and those that remained were caught in the Kiev pocket. Once Pavlov's command had disappeared in the Minsk pocket, he was summoned back to Moscow and shot.

The Red Army's only other medium tank was the cumbersome-looking T-28. This was in production by 1932 and was fitted with three turrets, one mounting a 45mm gun and the other two with machine guns. Despite carrying a crew of six and weighing almost 30 tons, it could still manage almost 25mph. This tank was not used operationally until 1939, by which stage the T-34 was well on its way. The T-35 heavy tank, weighing in at 45 tons, appeared in 1933 and was a similar-looking tank, although only about sixty were built. The Soviets also had thousands of light tanks that were not capable of taking on the panzers.

In the 1930s the bulk of the armour was the BT light fast tank. The main model was the BT-5 – a copy of the US Christie M-1931 but equipped with a larger cylindrical turret, a 45mm gun, a co-axial machine gun and a larger engine. With a crew of three and a weight of 11.5 tons, it could manage nearly 70mph on the road. The successor model, the BT-7, went into production in 1935. The single turret T-26B light tank appeared in 1933 (the earlier T-26A had twin turrets) and was also armed with a 45mm or 37mm gun. Its weight of 9 tons gave it a road speed of just 18mph;

Yet another flipped T-34 causes the advancing Wehrmacht some amusement.

The KV-1 went into service at the same time at the T-34. While the design was sound in principle, lack of numbers and training meant it suffered the same fate as its counterpart in 1941.

This Model 1941 turret shows just how exposed the interior was with the hatch open. In this instance it has been blown clean off, along with the turret.

A smashed and mangled Model 1941 with the 1942 cast turret. Behind it is an up-armoured KV-1, which has had additional armour bolted to the turret. This served to make the tank even heavier and cut down its manoeuvrability with predictable results.

This Model 1941 has the later cast turret and twin periscopes. Its position in the middle of a swamp indicates the ineptitude of the crew. The subsequent Model 1942 T-34/76 replaced the clumsy single hatch with separate hatches for the commander and gunner.

Another Model 1941 with the cast turret. As with most T-34s, the front track guards are bent out of shape and were easily torn off.

The interior of this Model 1941 seems a source of great fascination to these German troops. Note how the rear of the turret hangs over the engine grill.

this low speed and the tank's poor mobility compared to the BT-5 resulted in production being abandoned in the mid-1930s.

Hitler had extensive intelligence on these tanks, having established a special department to survey Russian industries, especially the weapons plants. In fact, his panzer troops already had experience of Soviet tanks thanks to the Hitler's involvement in the Spanish Civil War in 1936. Although the Germans had discovered that the Republican forces' Soviet-supplied T-26 tank was superior to their Panzer Mk I, the German 3.7cm Pak 35/36 anti-tank gun was found to penetrate 40mm of armour at 400 yards. The reality of the situation by the summer of 1941 was that the BT-5/7 and T-26 were obsolete and could simply not not cope with the firepower of Panzer Mk III and IV medium tanks or the *Sturmgeschütz* III assault gun, while the T-28 and heavy tanks like the T-35 and KV-1 were easily outmanoeuvred.

The brand-new T-34s first went into action at Grondno in Belorussia on the day of the invasion. Their appearance caught the Germans completely by surprise, but there were not enough of them, nor did the Soviets know how to use them effectively. Another of the T-34's first combat operations took place with the Red Army's 2nd Tank Division near Rassinye in Lithuania. About fifty tanks from the 3rd Tank Regiment sought to blunt the advance of the 1st and 6th Panzer Divisions on 24–25 June 1941. Initially the Germans were alarmed to find that their 37mm anti-tank rounds just bounced off the T-34's frontal armour, but the 88mm flak gun deployed in an anti-tank role rapidly brought the Soviets to a halt.

# Chapter Five

# **Moscow Miracle**

Following the successful evacuation of the Soviet tank-producing facilities east of the Urals during 1941, production of the T-34 was conducted at Chelyabinsk and Nizhny Tagil as well as at a number of other subsidiary plants well out of the reach of the Luftwaffe. However, at the outbreak of war T-34 production was far from centralised and was spread over vast distances. The Kirov factory manufactured the L-11 gun in Leningrad, while electrical components were made in Moscow at the Dinamo Factory. The tanks themselves were initially built in 1940 in Kharkov at the No. 183 Factory; this was supplemented by tank production at the Stalingrad Tractor Factory (STZ) in early 1941, then in the middle of that year the Krasnoye Sormovo Factory No. 112 in Gorkiy also began to manufacture T-34s.

Kharkov could not produce enough V-2 diesel engines for the tanks, which resulted in the Gorkiy T-34s having to be fitted with the BT tank's Mikulin M-17T gasoline aero engine and a substandard clutch and transmission. These tanks were to prove troublesome when the fighting started. Likewise radios were in short supply and were only installed in company commander's tanks – the rest of the company had to rely on flags for communication. Production of the F-34 gun was undertaken firstly at Gorkiy and then at Kharkov as well. Operation Barbarossa – Hitler's attack on the Soviet Union – not surprisingly swiftly focused Stalin's attention on the T-34 production lines.

After Hitler's invasion, Stalin sought to safeguard his factories and established the Peoples' Commissariat for Tank Production. Most of the Soviet defence plants, including their tank production facilities, only just escaped Hitler's grasp. General Georgi Zhukov marvelled at what he called the 'Russian miracle': the swift dismantling and relocation of the Soviet Union's factories out of harm's way. In total, around 1,300 major industrial enterprises were evacuated to the east. Before long these factories were churning out replacement T-34/76s and then the new improved version known as the T-34/85, with its thicker frontal armour to withstand German anti-tank guns.

Hitler's remarkable victory in the summer of 1941 was due to his efficient use of panzers, the speed of the operation, high morale and overall superior equipment. Nonetheless the new T-34/76, once fine-tuned, was not found wanting, causing an

A burnt-out Model 1941 or 1942 lies in the winter snow, having rear-ended another tank. It was during the winter of 1941/42 that the T-34 began to show what it was capable of in the defence of Moscow. However, they were still too few in number and the Germans had more pressing concerns, such as the lack of cold weather clothing and widespread frostbite.

Another Model 1941/42 during the winter. This is a good ambush position but the crew would have been freezing.

acceleration in German tank design to try to counter it. The T-34 was well suited to the Russian weather; in particular, its wide tracks and low ground pressure gave it good traction and speed. What the Red Army needed was replacement tanks and quickly, before Hitler renewed his push on Moscow.

New tank plants sprang up east of the Ural Mountains, notably Uralvagonzavod in Nizhny Tagil and the Tractor Factory at Chelyabinsk, which had to make good the appalling losses. The tank factory at Kharkov was evacuated to Nizhny Tagil to help create Ural Tank Factory No. 183. Likewise Kharkov's diesel engine factory and Leningrad's Kirov Plant (Factory No. 100) and S.M. Kirov (No. 185) moved to Chelyabinsk and combined with the Tractor Factory to became popularly known as 'Tankograd' or 'Tank City'. Leningrad's Voroshilov Plant (Factory No. 174) moved to Chkalov in 1941 and then to Omsk in 1942.

According to Zhukov, the first batch of T-34s were delivered from the Chelyabinsk production line just a month after the relocation of the Leningrad factory. The Krasnoye Sormovo shipyards in Gorkiy on the Volga were also put to work producing T-34 tanks, and these were employed during the Battle of Moscow

The Red Army preparing to defend Moscow. Stalin launched a counterattack that only just succeeded in holding the Germans.

(*Opposite, top*) Muscovites digging tank ditches in an attempt to stop the panzers' drive on Moscow.

(*Opposite, below*) Zhukov was ordered by Stalin to counterattack before Moscow, but, lacking sufficient resources, particularly tanks, he struggled in this task. Many Model 1941s such as this one were needlessly sacrificed.

# Colour Plates

These colour plates were produced by graphic artist David Hemingway to give a general impression of the paint schemes employed on the T-34, SU-85 and SU-122 between 1941 and 1945. The emphasis is on 'general' as Red Army tank crews tended to be a law unto themselves when in the field.

The basic colours used on Red Army vehicles comprised 4BO, a very dark olive green, 6K, a dark brown or black, and 7K, a sand/ochre. The green was composed of yellow ochre (40–60 per cent), zinc chromate (15–20 per cent), white (10–20 per cent) and ultramarine (8–13 per cent). 6K (or 6RP) is believed to have been a rich dark brown or black. The 7K was a green-yellow, which actually came out sand grey. In 1942 Soviet tank camouflage guidelines stipulated 50 per cent of the surface area be painted with 4BO, with 25 per cent for each of the 6K and 7K.

In reality, these colours, once applied, varied enormously. The paints were issued as a paste and diluted by up to 50 per cent with thinner – this inevitably impacted on the final colour once dry. In addition, it has been asserted that 4BO actually darkened with time as a result of a chemical reaction. Normally colour fades with prolonged exposure to bright sunlight.

There has been much debate over the level of camouflage used on Red Army armoured fighting vehicles and there does not seem to have been standardisation across the various Soviet 'fronts'. The different Soviet military districts utilised varying colour combinations depending on the local geographic conditions. Leningrad, Moscow and others all the way down to the Caucasus developed camouflage schemes using three colours over the base green but this was tailored to local conditions (for more detailed guidance on this, see 'Colour Schemes and Camouflage', pp. 41–4).

During the winter Soviet tank crews used zinc white or titanium white with an oil base with small amounts of ultramarine colouring as the base colour. In the absence of oil-based paint, the crews resorted to using powdered chalk mixed with water. The only snag with the latter was that it was not colour-fast and washed off easily; as a result, the effectiveness of whitewashing varied considerably.

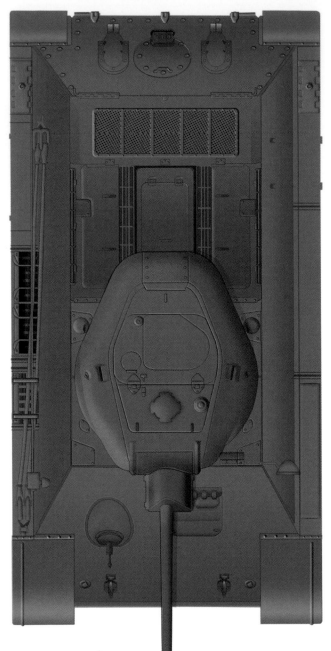

**T-34/76B**

This Model 1941 or T-34/76B is in the Red Army's standard dark olive green. Visible on the top view are the warm air extraction vents either side of the V-2 engine and grill over the transmission housing, containing the main clutch, brakes, electric starter, final drives, gearbox, ventilators, and two main fuel tanks. This layout was standard on the T-34/76, T-34/85 and the tank destroyer variants.

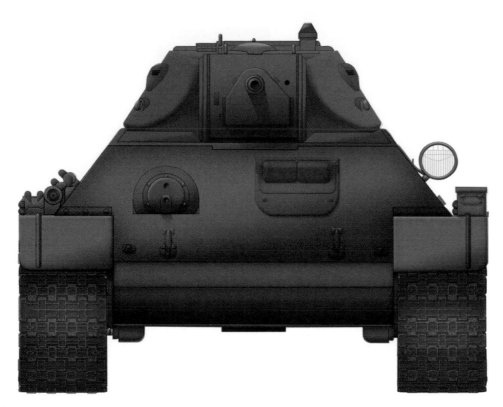

On the rear view note the armoured housing covering the downward-facing exhaust outlets and the circular transmission access hatch. The latter was square on the initial T-34/76A Model 1940 and on some T-34/76Bs, but round on all subsequent variants, including the T-34/85 and tank destroyers.

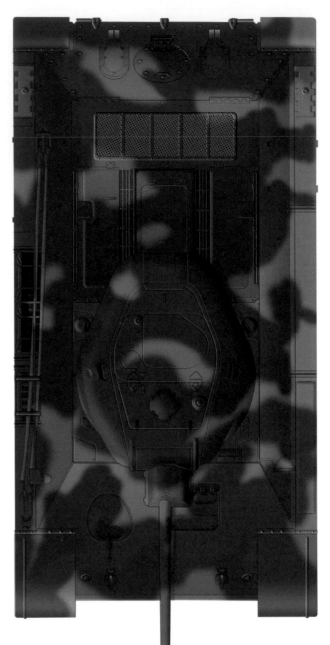

## T-34/76B

A T-34/76B depicted in a three-tone camouflage scheme, which was either sprayed or brushed on. As the war progressed, this was abandoned in favour of a green base coat. As a general rule, the Model 1940/1941 T-34s had solid rubber-rimmed road wheels and the Model 1942/1943s had solid and spoke rubber-rimmed road wheels, as well as spoke metal-rimmed ones.

From the Model 1941 onwards some T-34/76 turrets had twin periscopes for both the commander and loader, but wartime shortages often meant the loader's periscope was omitted, as here. Likewise, the T-34/76D Model 1943 only had a commander's periscope.

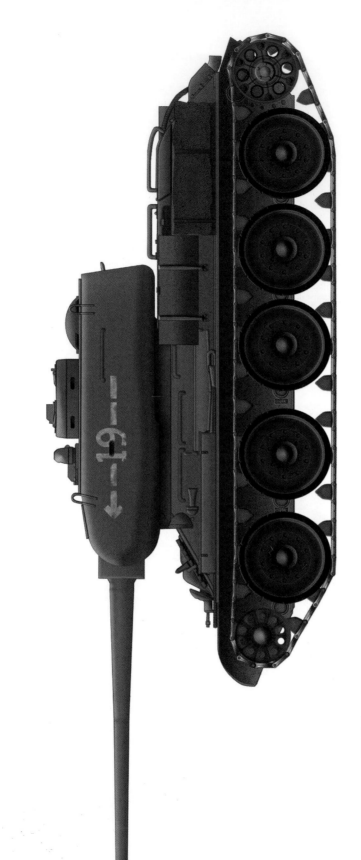

## T-34/85

The T-34/85 was either painted dark olive green or whitewashed depending on the season. White unit numbers and horizontal lines on the turret were common. The rear deck layout is the same as on the T-34/76.

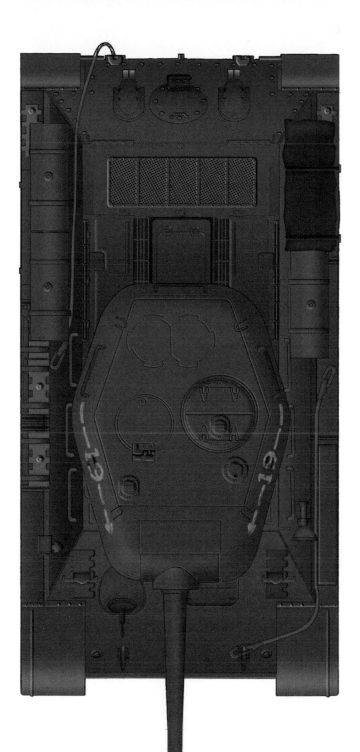

This view shows the much higher profile of the T-34/85 compared to the T-34/76. Inevitably, the larger turret presented a much better target. The turret has twin hatches, twin ventilator domes fore and aft and three periscopes.

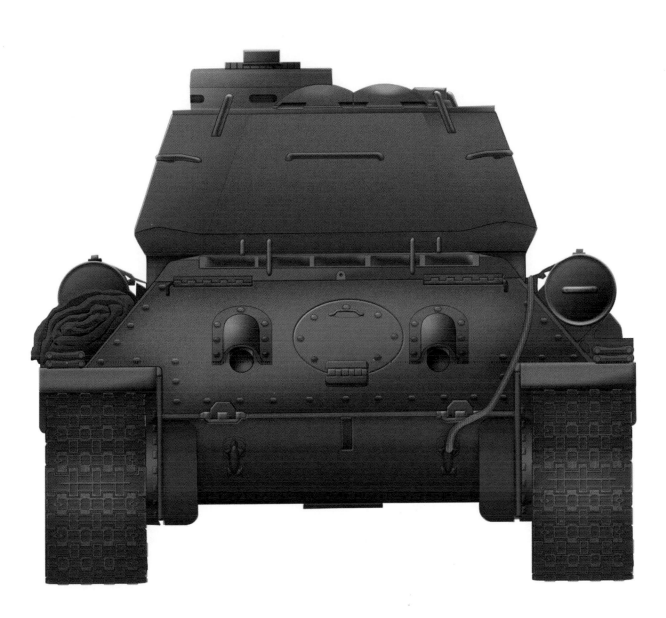

## SU-122

The SU-122 tank destroyer looked formidable, but the low velocity of the 122mm howitzer made it a poor anti-tank weapon.

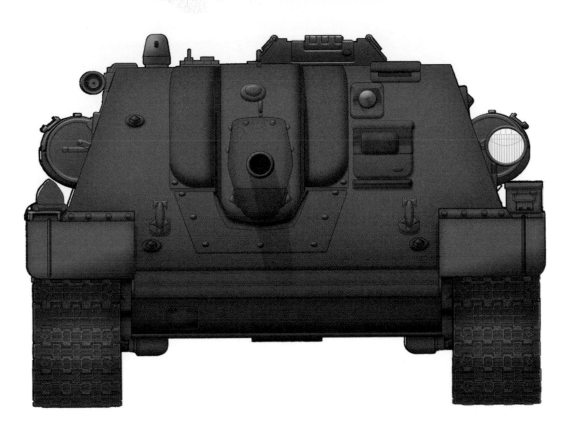

The SU-122 retained the standard T-34 chassis but replaced the turret with a large fighting compartment to house the howitzer. Aiming the weapon required manoeuvring the entire vehicle.

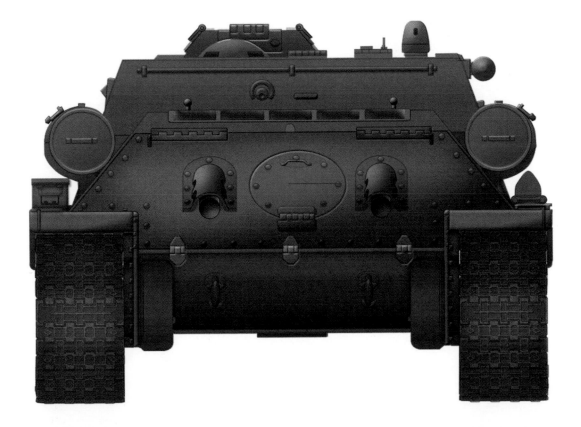

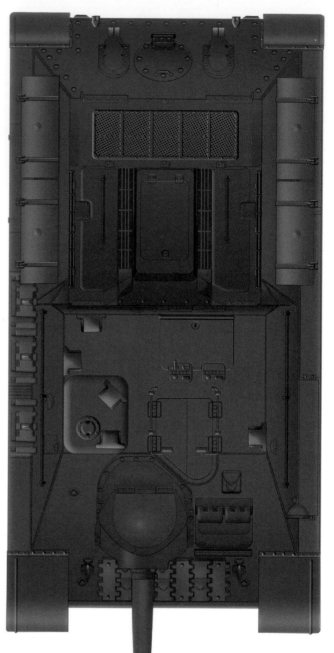

**SU-85**

The SU-85 tank destroyer armed with the 85mm anti-tank gun was better than the SU-122 but was rapidly superseded by the T-34/85.

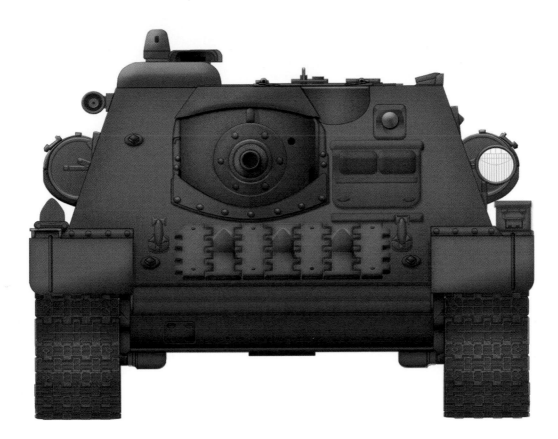

The SU-85 and SU-100 were very similar but the latter had a much longer gun barrel, greatly reducing manoeuvrability.

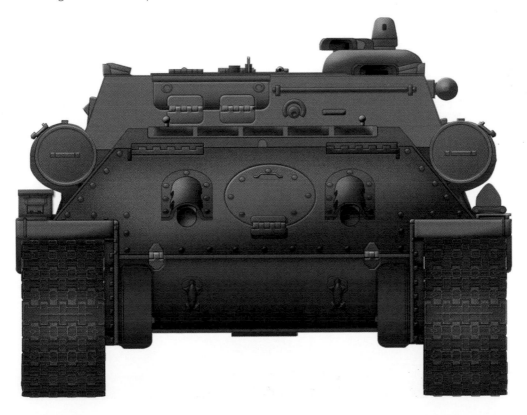

Cobbaton Combat Collection's Model 1945/1946 T-34/85. This particular example was supplied to the Czech Army and was to have fought in the Arab–Israeli Wars with the Egyptians but was never delivered.

The finish on the T-34/85 was no frills: note the highly crude casting on both the turret sides and the turret mantlet. In wartime, grinding a smooth finish on the castings and the welds was not a priority.

The plug for the pistol port is held in place by an interior weighted cable.

These spare track links on the turret handrail show how the simple pin connector works.

On the right are the flywheel and fan, with the ring gear to the left for the starter to engage; the end of the starter is visible centre top. At the bottom is the drive shaft through to the gearbox that is on the left.

V-2 transmission and gear housing. In the centre are the flywheel and fan with the starter ring gear and the upper pipe work; the two circular objects are the twin Cyclone air filters. Below them are the exhausts. The steel shutters can be unbolted to give better access.

View looking from the turret rearward through the engine inspection hatch into the 'V' of the V-2 engine.

The diesel injection pump for the twelve cylinders, with the yellow diesel pipes leading to the two valve rocker covers, left and right in this view, and then through them into the cylinder heads. The two blue vertical parts are the inlet manifolds, drawing air from the two Cyclone air cleaners under the rear of the engine deck. Top of the picture is the engine coolant filler cap with two green pipes leading left and right to the two radiators.

The V-2 viewed from the T-34/85 fighting compartment. On the left, the black and brown vertical cylinder is the electric oil pump, for priming the engine lubrication system before starting. The crab-like item in the centre, with the blue pipes radiating from it, is the engine air-starting distributor. Bottom right in brown is the oil control tap. The various yellow pipes are all fuel pipes. (The colour scheme for pipes is: brown: engine oil, blue: air, yellow: diesel fuel, and green: engine coolant water).

Germans troops with a captured 1941/42 T-34 with a cast turret.

in December 1941. Zhukov, who was charged with defending the capital, noted that the tanks came just in time, though there were not enough for his liking. He told Stalin he needed 200 additional tanks, but he did not get them.

On the road to Moscow the Germans encountered the KV-1 and the T-34 and rapidly realised that their panzers were now outgunned and under-armoured. The wake-up call came on 6 October 1941 when Heinz Guderian's 2nd Panzer Army ran into a brigade of T-34s under Colonel General Mikhail Katukov near Mtensk. The T-34s knocked out ten Panzer Mk III and IVs for the loss of only five of their own number. It was evident that the Germans' short 50mm and 75mm anti-tank guns could only penetrate the T-34's sloping frontal armour from the almost suicidal distance of 100m. In contrast, the T-34 could kill the Panzer Mk III and IV at 1,000m. On top of this, while the panzers were struggling with the ice and mud of the Russian winter, the T-34s were able to plough ahead regardless, thanks to their wide tracks. Only the German 88mm flak gun could stop the T-34 at range.

Once it became clear that the 20,000 tanks of the Red Army had all but disappeared in the summer of 1941, all thoughts of the new T-34M design were shelved and the Model 1941 became the standard production model, with another 1,886 built during the last six months of 1941. Even this, though, was not enough as 2,300 tanks were lost in trying to stave off the Nazis. Once the Kharkov production line had been shifted to Nizhny Tagil, work was undertaken to simplify the design with the Model 1942; this also saw the frontal armour increased to 65mm, which

German troops surveying the results of one of Zhukov's counterattacks. The tank in the background has the metal-rimmed wheels.

added another 2 tons to the tank's weight. The shortcomings of the KV-1 meant that the T-34 was the only effective tank in production. As tank building was cranked up, some 12,553 tanks rolled off the production line in 1942, although more than 50 per cent became casualties of war.

The incredible rate of tank production was in part due to the portable fusion welder designed by mechanical engineer Yevgeny Paton. Nikita Khruschev recalled: 'Thanks to the improvements he introduced in our tank production, tanks started coming off our assembly lines like pancakes off a griddle. . . . He moved with our armour works to the Urals when we had to evacuate our industry from Kharkov early in the war.'

On 14 November 1941 Stalin, desperate to forestall Hitler, instructed Zhukov to conduct spoiling attacks south of Moscow and around Volokolamsk, but Zhukov was reluctant to waste his precious reserves of tanks on an enterprise that was unlikely to produce positive results. General Rokossovsky's 16th Army, which had been busy preparing in-depth defences, was instructed to leave its sanctuary. Pushing forward just a mile, it suffered heavy casualties. Rokossovsky held Zhukov personally responsible for these needless losses.

On 18 November a Soviet division newly arrived from the Far East and supported by an armoured brigade attacked the German 112th Infantry Division guarding the 4th Panzer's push on Venev. The 112th, having already suffered 50 per cent casualties to frostbite, was overrun by T-34 tanks. A week later German intelligence identified more fresh reserves from the Far East – the 108th Tank

Brigade and the 31st Cavalry and 299th Rifle Divisions; all were thrown into the fighting.

By the end of the month Zhukov was more than satisfied with the Red Army's efforts to defend Moscow, claiming:

In twenty days of the second phase of their offensive, the Germans lost 155,000 dead and wounded, 800 tanks, at least 300 guns and 1,500 planes. The heavy losses, the complete collapse of the plan for a blitzkrieg ending to the war, and the failure to achieve their strategic objectives depressed the spirit of the German forces and gave rise to the first doubts about a successful outcome of the war. The Nazi military–political leadership also lost its reputation of 'invincibility' before world public opinion.

On 2 December 1941 von Kluge's 4th Army was launched into the attack and advanced elements of the 258th Infantry Division actually penetrated Moscow's suburbs. Strong Soviet counterattacks convinced von Kluge that he was not going to break through and that these advanced units should be withdrawn. This proved to be a prudent move as Zhukov threw a hundred divisions into his general counteroffensive.

Zhukov was acutely aware that his counteroffensive was deficient in tanks and aircraft:

Late in the evening of 4 December the Chief [Stalin] telephoned me and asked, 'Is there anything else you need beyond what we gave you?'
I said I still needed air support from Supreme Headquarters reserve and the air defence forces and at least 200 tanks and crews. The front had too few tanks and needed more for the rapid development of the counteroffensive.
'We can't give you any tanks; we don't have any,' Stalin said. 'But you'll get your air support. Arrange it with the General Staff. I am going to call them now. Just remember that the Kalinin Front offensive begins on 5 December and the operational group on the right wing of the South West Front around Yelets on the 6th.'

Zhukov's available T-34s rolled round the Germans' positions, deliberately avoiding any centres of resistance, in order to push as far as possible into the enemy's rear. Panzer commander Major-General F.W. von Mellenthin recalled, 'In 1941 we had nothing comparable with the T-34, with its 50mm maximum armour, 76mm high-velocity gun, and its relatively high speed with splendid cross-country performance. These tanks were not thrown into battle in large numbers until our spearheads were

Workers prepare to install a turret using a massive gantry.

More Model 1943 tanks on the production lines. These are readily identifiable by the hexagonal and flat-fronted turret with twin hatches.

The evacuation of the Soviet Union's tank plants to Chelyabinsk to create Tankograd was called the 'Russian miracle' by Zhukov. This move compensated for the restricted production at Leningrad and the loss of plants at Kharkov and Stalingrad. This production line is assembling the T-34/76D Model 1943.

Ready for action. These crews are collecting whitewashed T-34/76Ds straight from the factory floor.

During the winter of 1942/43 Hitler's allies, tasked with defending his flanks at Stalingrad, had no answer to the T-34 that swiftly cut through their lines. This T-34/76D seems to have very faded whitewash. The panel on the turret is probably a painted-on Soviet flag.

A knocked-out T-34/76D Model 1943 exposed by the spring thaw. The rear of the hexagonal turret shows how the shot trap had been greatly reduced.

approaching Moscow; they then played a great part in saving the Russian capital.'

By the time of Zhukov's counteroffensive, the German Army had suffered more than 100,000 cases of frostbite. On 5 December Hitler's offensive was formally called off; two days earlier some local withdrawals had already been sanctioned. The net result was that Zhukov held Moscow, thanks in no small part to the T-34.

Despite the Soviet Union's massive losses, it had 7,700 tanks by the beginning of 1942 and 20,600 by the following year. Soviet tank factories were churning out 2,000 a month, rising to almost 3,000 by the end of 1943. In the summer of 1942 the Soviets abandoned their earlier tactics and began to form entire tank armies, with armoured and mechanised corps.

Emboldened by their success before Moscow, the Red Army attempted to recapture Kharkov in April 1942, but lack of experience once again played in the panzers' favour. A German counterattack resulted in fourteen Soviet tank brigades, largely equipped with T-34s, being scattered. It was a terrible waste of resources, but was symptomatic of Stalin's impatience to push back the Nazi invaders before the Red Army had fully recovered and rearmed.

# Chapter Six

# T-34s in Ukraine

The turning point on the Eastern Front came in 1943. By the middle of the year General Vannikov's tank factories were out-producing the panzers by nearly 3:1. A total of 15,812 T-34/76 tanks were built in 1943, with monthly production at around 1,300 a month. Such a production rate is hard to credit. The T-34's immediate foes, the Panther and Tiger, made up only about 41 per cent of German panzer production in 1943, with the Panzer Mk IV remaining the backbone of Hitler's *Panzerwaffe*. During 1943 the Red Army lost over 14,000 T-34/76s, including some 6,000 expended in the battle with Army Group South from July to December that year. Crucially though, Soviet production was keeping pace with the Red Army's tank losses.

In mid-1942 Morozov came up with the Model 1943, which incorporated the hexagonal turret with two hatches instead of the heavier single one on the earlier models. This turret also had thicker armour at 70mm but visibility issues were not solved until a cupola was fitted in mid-1943. The Model 1943 T-34 comprised the bulk of the T-34s deployed in Ukraine in the summer of 1943. This need to keep on pouring out high volumes of tanks showed that Soviet tank design had all but stagnated – the T-34 was still armed with the 76.2mm gun and was increasingly vulnerable to the improved German anti-tank guns.

The T-34/76 had been intended to withstand German anti-tank guns in the 37mm–50mm calibre range, but things changed when the Panzer Mk IV F2 appeared in May 1942 armed with the 75mm KwK 40 L-43 gun. This could take on the T-34 at a range of 1,000m, giving the panzers a much-needed stand-off capability to help them cope with superior Soviet tank numbers.

By 1943 the T-34's F-34 tank gun was out of date. Its standard armour-piercing round could penetrate the Panther's side armour at 1,000m, but could only tackle the glacis armour at some 300m and it could not get through the frontal armour of the turret. This meant that the Red Army fighting in Ukraine was supported by a tank that no longer enjoyed any real technical advantage over the panzers. One saving grace was that by 1943 the T-34's durability allowed the Soviet tank units to enjoy a 70–90 per cent reliability rate – in contrast, German units equipped with the Panther could manage only half this figure.

During the winter of 1942/43 the T-34 started to contribute to Soviet victories, most notably at Stalingrad. This T-34/76D has a very crude and streaky application of whitewash or diluted chalk — nonetheless it has had the desired effect. The tank has a mix of rubber and steel-rimmed wheels.

Further compounding the T-34 crews' woes, their armour had been increased from 45mm to only 75mm, whereas 90mm was required to offer protection against the KwK 40. The low nickel content of Soviet plate armour meant it had a nasty habit of spalling when hit. This would send steel splinters flying around the inside of the tank, causing appalling injuries to the crew.

At Kursk Hitler pinned his hopes on the upgunned Panzer Mk IV and Panther armed with a high-velocity 75mm gun and the Tiger armed with an 88mm gun killing vast numbers of T-34s. While the Soviets sought to win the war using a simple and well rounded tank design, the Germans opted for producing a series of different tanks, as well as numerous armoured fighting vehicles that had specified roles as self-propelled guns, assault guns and tank destroyers. While the latter found a use for the chassis of the more obsolete of the panzers, it meant that production was never solely dedicated to the Panzer Mk IV, the Tiger and the Panther. The Germans

General Pavel Rotmistrov, commanding the 7th Tank Corps, poses with a whitewashed Model 1943. He subsequently commanded the powerful 5th Guards Tank Army during the battle of Kursk in 1943 and Operation Bagration in 1944.

This photograph very graphically illustrates the problem of driving over powdery snow at speed – such plumes of snow would soon attract attention from enemy gunners. Prior to an attack, crews were instructed to drive slowly to their jumping-off points.

In 1942 a new type of T-34 was produced. Designated the T-34/76C, it had a larger cast turret, webbed and spudded tracks and two small hatches.

desperately sought a technical solution to their predicament on the Eastern Front but this simply slowed up production, especially in the case of the Tiger, which was time-consuming to manufacture. The Soviets on the other hand realised that the T-34 was as good as they were going to get in the interim and opted to delay a modernisation programme in favour of replacing their shattered tank fleet as swiftly as possible. The upgunned T-34/85 was not ready until 1944, by which time the Red Army already had the upper hand.

In the summer of 1943 these contrasting approaches to armoured warfare went head to head in Ukraine, which offered by far the best open terrain for tanks. Here tanks, anti-tank mines and anti-tank guns came together in a vast and deadly killing ground. The German generals understood that if they could contain the Red Army in Ukraine and fight it to a standstill, then there was a chance of victory – or at least some sort of ceasefire. At the same time the Soviet generals knew that the course of the Second World War depended on the outcome in Ukraine. If they could defeat Hitler's panzer armies there, then the road to Eastern Europe and Nazi Germany would be open.

After the shock of the German invasion in the summer of 1941, the Soviet high command sought to learn from its Moscow counteroffensive in the winter of 1941/42. What was clear was that they needed tanks – a lot of tanks – and so tank production became a priority. By the spring of 1942 the Soviets had begun to form

A knocked-out Model 1941 or 1942.

The T-34/76B is distinguishable by the single hatch and roll plate armour on the turret. Judging by the soil piled in front of the hull, it seems that this tank had been driven into a defensive position. The Soviets dug-in many of their tanks prior to the German attack against the Kursk salient.

Kursk was the turning point, and heralded the liberation of Ukraine. These poor-quality Soviet propaganda shots show T-34s in action in the summer of 1943; at first glance they look like T-34/85s, but the lack of a commander's cupola confirms they are T-34/76 Model 1943s.

German panzergrenadiers shelter beside a captured T-34/76D. The man standing by the tank is holding an anti-tank mine.

German troops inspect another knocked-out T-34. This tank was caught on an exposed raised road, typical of the open Russian steppe. By mid-1943 the Soviets were out-producing the panzers by 3:1; at such a ratio, the Germans simply could not destroy the T-34s fast enough.

As the Red Army rolled back the Wehrmacht, it was able to regain possession of many previously abandoned tanks, such as these Model 1941s.

In the winter of 1943 the Germans take stock of a captured column of T-34/76Ds.

Another T-34/76D, this time under tow with a Tiger. At Kursk the Tigers and the Panthers were simply swamped by the T-34s.

dedicated tank corps, followed by mechanised corps. The former consisted of one motorised and three tank brigades, the latter of one tank and three mechanised brigades, with both types fielding about 170 tanks. (Soviet organisational terminology is not the same as in Western armies. In the latter brigades make up a division; with the Soviets it was reversed. Rather confusingly, in manpower terms a Soviet division was roughly equivalent to a regiment or battalion.)

The first Soviet tank armies, the 3rd and the 5th, appeared in the spring of 1942. Designed as breakthrough forces, these new tank armies and corps were blooded at Kharkov, on the Bryansk front, on the Voronezh front and on the approaches to Stalingrad. To start with, their deployment was a case of trial and error, more often than not resulting in heavy losses as they fell foul of the panzers' superior tactics. Eventually, though, their growing confidence paid off, notably with good results at Stalingrad, where the T-34 cut through the ill-equipped Hungarian, Italian and Romanian armies guarding the flanks to trap the German 6th Army.

At the beginning of 1943 the Soviets took the decision to create five standardised tank armies, all of which contributed to their decisive victory at Kursk. The T-34-based mineclearer also saw action at Kursk, where the 166th Separate Engineer Tank Regiment saw action with its eighteen PT-34 mine-rollers and twenty-two T-34 gun tanks.

It was at Prokhorovka during the battle of Kursk that the T-34 bested the Tiger and the Panther. On 12 July 1943 the tanks of General Pavel Rotmistrov's 5th Tank Army engaged the panzers at very close range in order to fire on their side and rear armour. The German 4th Panzer Army lost 300 panzers, including no fewer than seventy Tigers, at Prokhorovka. In return, the Red Army lost about 400 tanks but Soviet industrial might quickly made good these losses. The Soviet forces were also left in possession of the battlefield, which meant that many of the less heavily damaged T-34s could be salvaged. As a result, by the end of 1943 the German panzers in Ukraine were severely outnumbered by the Red Army's tank fleet.

Hitler had gambled on the Panther becoming a successful counter to the T-34 but the Panther had been rushed into production and rushed into combat and its crews paid the inevitable price. The Panther had achieved some tactical successes for the German Army, but it did little to change the overall strategic situation. During the fighting in Ukraine from July to December 1943 the Panthers claimed around 500 T-34s, or roughly 10 per cent of the Soviet tanks lost in Ukraine. The T-34 claimed only about a dozen Panthers destroyed, but the T-34 crews had kept the Panthers under pressure and on the move, which played havoc with their mechanical reliability. And by mid-1944 any advantages the Panther's gun may have initially offered were increasingly overshadowed by the Soviet 85mm and 122mm anti-tank guns. This was especially the case once the T-34/85 arrived on the battlefield.

# Chapter Seven

# T-34s in White Russia

During the spring of 1944 the Red Army's Guards armoured brigades were issued with the very first new T-34/85s. Once production was in full swing, it became the standard medium tank in all armoured units, although the T-34/76 remained in widespread service. While many units were re-equipped for the coming Bagration offensive, they did not all get the T-34/85, instead having to make do with the earlier 76.2mm-armed Model 1942/43s as battle replacements.

By the beginning of 1944, despite the massive losses sustained at Kursk and in Ukraine, thanks to Soviet industry the Red Army was still able to field 5,357 tanks and self-propelled guns. The six tank armies had nearly forty armoured corps. For the Byelorussia offensive in June that year the Soviets committed the bulk of their armoured forces, including five tank armies, plus ten separate tank and mechanised corps.

In addition, to reinforce the infantry, they deployed separate infantry brigades, self-propelled artillery and heavy tank regiments. The 6th Tank Army formed in January 1944 with about 600 tanks and self-propelled guns, 500 guns and mortars and 30,000 men. The tank corps each numbered 207 tanks and 63 self-propelled guns, whilst the mechanised corps could field 183 tanks and the same number of self-propelled guns.

Although originally intended to coincide with D-Day on 6 June 1944, Joseph Stalin's Operation Bagration did not commence until 0500 on the 23rd. It opened with a barrage that lasted for over two hours and penetrated to a depth of nearly 4 miles. For the first 15 minutes Red Army gunners furiously poured hot metal onto the German positions to a depth of 2 miles, and after that there was 90 minutes of fire directed at observed targets, artillery positions and weapons pits. There was also 20 minutes of a general bombardment against the Germans' main line of resistance and their rear areas.

For the troops of Hitler's Army Group Centre the density of this was truly shocking. Stalin's forces brought to bear no fewer than 24,000 guns and mortars along the 431-mile line. Up to 90 per cent of the artillery was deployed on the breakthrough sectors, which only represented up to 20 per cent of the overall width of the front under attack.

The bulk of the Red Army's tank forces in the summer of 1944 consisted either of the T-34/76D (seen here in the foreground) or the newer T-34/85 (at the rear of the column).

Cannon fodder: a T-34/76D Model 1943 burning in a ditch. This is one of the later versions fitted with the commander's cupola, so it may be a T-34/76E. Operation Bagration, which saw the destruction of Hitler's Army Group Centre, cost Stalin 2,957 tanks – the industrial might of 'Tankograd' would enable him to shrug off such losses.

This was to be no amphibious assault as in Normandy, but a massive armoured charge led by the T-34 across the length and breadth of the Soviet republic of Byelorussia or White Russia. Opposite Hitler's Army Group Centre were four Soviet Fronts; this meant that over 40 per cent of the entire Red Army was committed to Bagration. Stalin had mustered a staggering 118 rifle divisions, 8 tank and mechanised corps, 6 cavalry divisions, 13 artillery divisions and 14 air defence divisions. These forces, including support troops, numbered 1.7 million men – more than double the size of Army Group Centre.

Most notably, for the opening stages of the offensive Stalin's generals had massed 2,715 tanks and 1,355 assault guns – about six times the number deployed by Army Group Centre. The vast majority of them were T-34/76s, T-34/85s and SU-85s/100s. Nothing could withstand such brute force.

The PT-34 mine-roller played a leading role in Stalin's version of D-Day. One notable unit equipped with specialised armoured fighting vehicles was the 116th Separate Engineering Tank Regiment. Their vehicles were used to clear the way to the strategic Minsk–Moscow highway from Smolensk to Orsha. This area was heavily fortified and held by the powerful German 78th Sturm (Assault) Division. To counter this, the 11th Guards Army's attack towards Orsha was supported by special engineer and tank units tasked with breaching the thick defensive belts.

The attacking rifle divisions were preceded by armoured assault forces each led by a company of ten PT-34s followed by heavy tanks and assault engineer battalions. At least five regiments of OT-34 flamethrowers were also deployed during Bagration: the 148th and 253rd with the 3rd Byelorussian Front, the 40th with the 3rd Shock Army and the 119th and 166th with the 1st Byelorussian Front. The PT-34s had to contend with German minefields, barbed wire, anti-tank ditches, trenches and bunkers, all staunchly defended by the 78th Sturm Division, which, although an infantry unit, was effectively equipped like a panzergrenadier division and bolstered by StuG III assault guns. In addition, once they realised what the mine-rollers were doing, the German anti-tank gunners made them priority targets.

Throughout May and June 1944 Hitler had been misled by fake build-ups in the 3rd Ukrainian Front and 3rd Baltic Front areas, convincing him that Stalin's major attacks would take place in Ukraine or the Baltic States. However, many of Hitler's commanders were uneasy about maintaining the 'Byelorussian Balcony', as the exposed bulge in Army Group Centre's line was nicknamed. To no avail Field Marshal von Busch, commanding Army Group Centre, pleaded with Hitler to pull out of Byelorussia, or at least to 'shorten the line'.

Unfortunately the resulting smoke and early morning fog on 23 June 1944 greatly hampered the supporting air attacks by the Red Air Force. Only General Chernyakovsky's force enjoyed clear weather, allowing Pe-2 bombers to carry out

Army Group Centre was reliant on insufficient numbers of assault guns rather than panzers to hold the T-34 at bay. Despite losses such as these, German resistance was overwhelmed in the space of several weeks. Both these T-34s are Model 1943s.

A T-34/76D showing off its 'Mickey Mouse' ears.

This T-34/76D has been pressed into German service; how long they could make use of it would depend on the availability of spares and ammunition. There was also the constant danger of friendly fire.

160 sorties. The ground-attack Shturmoviks had to wait until the artillery and rocket launchers had finished their work. Afterwards the Soviet infantry surged forwards to seize tactical ground that could be exploited as a springboard for the impending breakthrough by the T-34s.

At 13.12 hours on 25 June General Gollwitzer, a German corps commander, signalled: 'Situation has changed. Completely encircled by constantly reinforcing enemy. 4th Luftwaffe Field Division exists no longer! 246th Infantry Division and 6th Luftwaffe Field Division in heavy combat on several fronts. Various penetrations into the city of Vitebsk. ...' Ominously at 15.00 hours Gollwitzer's HQ signalled: 'Situation at its climax.'

By early afternoon the Soviet 1st Tank Corps under General Butkov had reached the Dvina and taken a damaged bridge. In Chernyakovsky's sector Lyudnikov's 39th Army was also pushing on to the river; supported by some elements of the 43rd Army, it was assigned the task of destroying those German units trapped at Vitebsk. The Germans tried desperately to break through the Soviet cordon, launching twenty-five counterattacks on the 25th and a similar number the following day but without success.

Traut's men were used to, and even expecting, Soviet bombardments, but the ferocity of the shelling on the 23rd must have stunned even them. Minefields and barbed-wire belts were obliterated, sandbags torn asunder and scattered, weapon pits and trenches wrecked. Any weapons caught on the surface soon became so much twisted and useless pieces of steel. The hapless Germans then found

Another T-34/76D in German service. This tank also has the commander's cupola, as fitted to the T-34/85.

themselves under attack by the PT-34s as they ploughed a furrow through what remained of the German minefields. But the T-34 mine-rollers did not have it all their own way as they came up against the assault guns assigned to Traut's division, as well as his dug-in anti-tank guns.

The plan was that General K.N. Galitskiy's 11th Guards would overwhelm the German defences along the Moscow–Minsk highway, which would permit Marshal Pavel Rotmistrov's 5th Guards Tank Army to deploy. As the 11th Guards struggled against the determined German resistance, the 1st Guards Rifle Division pushed between Traut's forces and the 256th Infantry to the north. Galitskiy then pushed General Burdeyny's 2nd Guards Tanks Corps through this gap along a railway line.

A sense of panic began to overwhelm those Germans in Orsha; some units began to fall back but it was too late. Towards the end of the 26th Burdeyny's tanks swept north of the city and his T-34s rolling to the west caught a German train full of wounded being evacuated from Orsha and blew it from the rails. That night the 11th Guards and 31st Armies overran the city.

(*Above and opposite*) German soldiers with captured Model 1941 T-34s, both identifiable by the large single hatch. The first tank has a full complement of steel wheels, although most images tend to show a combination of metal and rubber. All-steel wheels were noisy and caused vibration on the metal tracks that was unpleasant for the crew and could cause physical damage to the tank.

A T-34/85 sweeps into Bucharest in 1944.

(*Opposite, top*) The T-34/76D proved popular with the crews. This preserved example has rubber-rimmed wheels.

(*Opposite, below*) A Model 1943 passing the smashed remains of a Panzer Mk IV.

General Zakharov's offensive opened with Grishin's attack north of Mogilev, supported by General K.A. Vershinin's 4th Air Army. As his men began crossing the Dnepr on the 26th, to the south General I.V. Boldin's 50th Army also thrust towards Mogilev. East of the city the tanks of the 33rd and 49th Armies hit the German 337th Infantry Division and broke through on the Ryassna–Mogilev road. Once the first and second German trench lines were breached, T-34s poured into the rear area of General Weidling's 39th Panzer Corps.

By the morning of the 27th General B.S. Bakarov's 9th Tank Corps had secured the Berezina crossings. General Rokossovsky, sensing that the time was right, now committed the 1st Guards Tank Corps and the 1st Mechanised Corps from Batov's 65th Army, sending them towards Baranovichi, southwest of Minsk. Rokossovsky's 1st Byelorussian Front trapped a sizeable number of German troops east of Bobruisk. Any German withdrawal or breakout attempt was now too late.

The fall of the defensive line Vitebsk–Orsha–Mogilev–Bobruisk meant that it was effectively all over for Army Group Centre. The entire German defensive system collapsed. By 30 June the first phase of the battle of Byelorussia was over; according to the Soviets, they had killed 132,000 Germans and took another 66,000 prisoner, as well as capturing or destroying 940 tanks, more than 5,000 guns and about 30,000 motor vehicles.

General M.F. Panov's 1st Guards Tank Corps from the 1st Byelorussian Front followed the T-34s of the 3rd Byelorussian Front to Minsk from the southeast. Minsk was liberated by the evening of 3 July and the people danced in the streets and rode on the tanks. In France the Allies would not liberate Paris until late August.

The near-total annihilation of Army Group Centre in the space of just under two weeks cost Hitler 300,000 dead, 250,000 wounded and about 120,000 taken prisoner. Stalin's losses included 2,957 tanks, 2,447 artillery pieces and 822 aircraft. His tank factories would enable him to shrug off such disastrous losses.

For Hitler, Bagration was a vastly more serious deathblow than the catastrophes at Stalingrad or in Normandy. The destruction of Army Group Centre was a bigger and swifter disaster than the loss of Army Group B's 7th Army and 5th Panzer Army at Falaise in mid-August 1944. Although overall total German losses in France were comparable to those in Byelorussia, the former occurred over a two-and-a-half month period, not in a matter of weeks. Stalin's D-Day was a formidable success, achieved in part by the T-34/76s and T-34/85s paving the way with German dead.

Nikolai Zheleznov, serving with the 4th Tank Army, recalled: 'The next operation in which I participated was the Lvov–Sandomierz offensive. I fought in a T-34/85 there. There were still only a few of them at that time – my platoon had just one. Our corps was sent to exploit the breakthrough. We marched towards Lvov, not encountering any resistance.'

# Chapter Eight

# T-34s on the Seelow Heights

The T-34 and SU-85/100, along with the newer IS-1 and IS-2 Joseph Stalin tanks, formed the bulk of the spearhead of the Red Army's assault on Berlin in 1945. First, though, they had to cross the Oder and overcome the German defences on the Seelow Heights. In securing these defensive positions Soviet tank losses were inevitably heavy, and even when the Red Army reached the streets and boulevards of the German capital the defenders resisted to the very last. Their defiance was to cost the Red Army no less than a third of its armoured forces.

The Seelow Heights were the key to Berlin's defences. The distinctive horseshoe-shaped Seelow plateau, rising up to 200ft in some places, lies west of Küstrin and overlooks the Oder flood-plain, a valley known as the Oderbruch. The attacking Red Army was funnelled up this valley and straight into Hitler's anti-tank guns.

From the very beginning the battle was a one-sided affair. For the Berlin offensive the Soviet 1st and 2nd Byelorussian and 1st Ukrainian Fronts fielded 2.5 million troops, equipped with some 6,250 tanks and self-propelled guns, and 41,600 artillery pieces and mortars, as well as 3,255 truck-mounted Katyusha rocket launchers and 7,500 aircraft. Zhukov hurled almost a million men of the 1st Byelorussian Front at the Seelow Heights. His assault commenced on 16 April 1945 with the usual massive bombardment of shells, rockets and bombs.

For this opening bombardment Zhukov joined General Chuikov, the commander of the 8th Guards Army. From his command post on the Reitwein Spur, Chuikov had the best view of the Seelow escarpment and the Oderbruch. He provided hot, strong tea, which Zhukov and his retinue drank in silence, preoccupied by thoughts of the 8,983 artillery pieces that were about to open fire. They had stockpiled 7 million shells and would expend 1,236,000 of them on the first day alone. The Red Air Force was also poised to launch 6,500 sorties.

The exposed heights and the town itself became a vast killing ground as the Soviet artillery and fighter-bombers sought out targets of opportunity. The Oder was breached before dawn by the T-34s of the 1st Byelorussian Front, while the tanks of the 1st Ukrainian Front barged across the Neisse. Captain Sergei Golbov, just north of Küstrin on the eastern bank of the flooded Oder, saw 'swarms of

Although the T-34 had been bolstered by the KV-85 and the KV-derived IS-1 and IS-2 Joseph Stalin heavy tanks, it was the T-34/85 that spearheaded the Red Army's assault on Berlin.

(*Opposite, top and below*) T-34/85s moving up for the attack. More than 6,200 tanks and self-propelled guns were massed for the offensive against Berlin. The Red Army first had to pierce the German defences on the Seelow Heights before it could reach the city.

A Soviet photograph showing T-34/85s supported by infantry. The Seelow Heights proved to be a killing ground for both sides.

assault troops, lines of tanks, platoons of engineers with sections of pontoon bridges and rubber boats. Everywhere the bank of the river was jammed with men and equipment and yet there was complete silence.'

In a series of telephone calls Stalin made it clear to Zhukov that if his forces did not breach the defences, then the honour of taking Berlin would be granted to Konev, who was pushing up from the south against the 4th Panzer Army. An irate Zhukov now gave the task of piercing the Seelow defences to Colonel General Mikhail Katukov's Soviet 1st Guards Tank Army.

Throwing the 1st and 2nd Guards Tank Armies into the fight did not immediately have the desired effect. The original plan was that they would exploit the breakthrough, not achieve it. Lacking space to manoeuvre, largely due to the swampy terrain, the T-34s had to use the roads, which were already packed with infantry. This created major traffic jams and provided the German anti-tank gunners with some prime targets. Predictably, the German artillery caught the T-34s and artillery struggling along the Oderbruch. Even when the tanks did reach the escarpment, they found the gradient too steep and were knocked out in great numbers.

General Busse's German 9th Army weathered three days of preliminary attacks on the Seelow Heights and then spent twenty-four hours enduring the full fury of Zhukov's assault. They knocked out more than 150 Soviet tanks and shot down 132 planes but it was not enough. The T-34s finally swarmed across the Seelow towards Berlin. Zhukov remarked:

At 1.50pm on 20 April the long-range artillery of the 79th Rifle Corps of the 3rd Assault Army commanded by Colonel General V.I. Kuznetsov was the first

This is what confronted the T-34 crews during their assault on Berlin: a massive anti-tank ditch with dragon's teeth, protected by minefields, anti-tank weapons and panzers.

The Soviet tank crews also had to contend with concrete bunkers and pillboxes. These were defended by German infantry armed with a variety of anti-tank weapons.

A T-34/76 standing guard on the streets of Berlin. By 26 April 1945 the 1st Guards Tank Army had fought its way through the southern suburbs.

to open fire on Berlin, thereby starting the historic storming of the German capital. On 21 April units of the 3rd Assault, 2nd Guards Tank, and 47th Armies entered the outskirts of Berlin and began the struggle in the city....

Ultimately, nothing could withstand Zhukov's armoured steamroller as it barged its way through the city. General Weidling later told his captors: '20 April was the hardest day for my Corps and probably for all the German troops. They had suffered tremendous losses in previous fighting; they were worn down and exhausted, and were no longer able to resist the tremendous thrust of the superior Russian forces.'

Despite being on the cusp of victory, the T-34s and SU-100s did not have it all their own way. On the streets of Berlin the T-34 crews were confronted by not only panzers and anti-tank weapons, but also mines, Molotov cocktail petrol bombs and tank-buster teams, often recruited from impressionable Hitler Youth armed with Panzerfausts. The latter made use of the city's tunnels and sewers to pop up in unexpected places and catch unwary tankers. At street junctions T-34 crews were caught by fire from emplaced 75mm and 88mm anti-tank guns, or set off mines or had petrol bombs dropped on them from the surrounding buildings. To avoid ambushes, Soviet tanks often simply drove through buildings, bringing them crashing down along with the defenders and any cowering residents.

T-34/85 crews, relishing their moment of triumph over Nazi Germany, posed for the camera in front of Berlin's iconic Brandenburg Gate. The grilles on the hull and turret were intended to deflect petrol bombs and Panzerfaust rounds.

Another T-34/85 by the Brandenburg Gate.

War's end. Swarming with jubilant infantry, tank crew and civilians, a T-34/85 rumbles through the streets of Prague in May 1945.

On the 26th Chuikov's 8th Guards Army and the 1st Guards Tank Army fought their way through the southern suburbs and attacked Tempelhof Airport, just inside the S-Bahn defensive ring. That very night the Soviets commenced shelling the Reichschancellery building, where Hitler was sheltering in the bunker built in the adjacent gardens. The Red Army was less than a mile away from its final destination. By the 27th the T-34s and their accompanying infantry were at Potsdamer Platz, just a few hundred yards from Hitler's bunker. Inside, Hitler was still waiting for General Walther Wenck's 12th Army, which was fighting on the Elbe, to come to Berlin's relief. On 30 April, seeing no prospect of help, Hitler committed suicide and shortly afterwards Germany surrendered. The T-34s' final moment of triumph came when T-34/85 crews stopped before Berlin's Brandenburg Gate to have their photographs taken.

# Chapter Nine

# T-34 Tank Aces

The summer of 1941 was a complete disaster for Stalin's armoured and mechanised forces. Hitler's highly experienced *panzertruppen* ran rings round the bewildered Soviet tankers. Stalin's massive tank force, albeit largely obsolete, simply vanished from the Red Army's order of battle as the tanks were knocked out, abandoned or trapped in the vast pockets created by the Wehrmacht's highly effective blitzkrieg.

The new T-34 was too few in number and its crews too inexperienced to make any difference to the overall outcome of the battle. Engine and transmission problems and a lack of ammunition compounded their woes. The Germans photographed T-34s that had overturned or driven into one another or plunged into rivers and marshes as the novice crews desperately sought to escape the attentions of the Luftwaffe, the German artillery and the panzers. Equally shaming for the Red Army was the fact that some of these mishaps had occurred as the crews, with no understanding of the T-34's capabilities, attempted to move into position to counterattack. There was no more humiliating sight than the Soviet Union's latest battle tank needlessly up to its hull in water, the engine flooded. Some might have argued that this was a criminal waste of resources, and indeed some generals paid for their ineptitude in front of a firing squad.

The one lesson the Soviets did learn from the disastrous tank battles of the summer of 1941 was the imperative of having well trained tank crews. The quality of a tank unit's fighting capabilities depended on a combination of the tank itself, crew training, tactical training and logistical support. Despite the terrible losses in 1941, enough tank crews survived the ordeal to provide a combat-hardened cadre that would form the backbone of the next generation of recruits. While the workers in the Soviet Union's tank factories strove to keep increasing their output, the tank training schools had to keep up with the demand for new crews.

Once the Soviet Union's tank factories had been relocated out of reach of the enemy, tank training regiments were established at Chelyabinsk, Nizhny Tagil and Sverdlovsk. Tank schools were also located at Kurgan, Ufa, Ulyanovsk and Saratov. Soviet crews normally spent up to eight weeks receiving basic training with a tank

German troops examining a captured T-34/76B or Model 1941, identifiable by the rolled plate turret and single hatch. Judging by its pristine condition, it had only just entered service before falling into German hands.

training battalion. They were then sent to a tank training regiment near one of the factories. These regiments could produce about 2,000 crewmen a month, but many of the men were often diverted to the factories, which were constantly short of labour. Once issued with their tanks, a march company of about ten vehicles conducted firing trials and then proceeded to the nearest railhead. The company was then shipped to the front to join its assigned tank battalion.

During the battles of 1941–42 the inexperienced tank crews paid a heavy price. Those who survived the winter battles of 1942/3 formed an important cadre of battle-hardened tank crews who would make all the difference at Kursk.

One man who stood out as a shining light in those dark days was the inspirational Senior Lieutenant Dimitry Fyodorovich Lavrinenko, who served with the 1st Guards Tank Brigade, 15th Tank Division. During 1941 he showed what could be achieved

This photograph clearly illustrates the shot trap caused by the turret overhang on the T-34/76B and C.

with the T-34/76 when it was used properly and he became the highest-scoring Allied tank ace of the war. Reportedly of Kuban Cossack stock, Lavrinenko completed his crew training in May 1938 at the Ulyanovsk Tank Academy. He subsequently took part in the invasions of eastern Poland in 1939 and Bessarabia the following year. This gave him and his comrades some idea of the capabilities of the T-26 and BT-7.

By the time of Operation Barbarossa Lavrinenko's unit had been equipped with the T-34/76. Employing the tank to its optimum, in the space of two-and-a-half months' fighting against the Nazi invaders he destroyed fifty-two panzers. Lavrinenko's mounting tally was only curtailed when he was killed on 18 December 1941 at the age of 27. While his total number of victories was relatively small compared to some of the German tank aces (such as Michael Wittmann, who destroyed 138 tanks and self-propelled guns), Lavrinenko's score was not surpassed by any other Allied tanker. For his achievements he was posthumously awarded the title of Hero of the Soviet Union on 5 May 1990. Even if Soviet propagandists had

One previous owner! German mechanics photographed with a 1942-built T-34/76B. This differed from the previous models in that the turret was cast, but it retained the single hatch. T-34 fought T-34 at Kursk. Note the two compressed air cylinders for cold starting have been removed, presumably for refilling.

(*Opposite, top*) Another captured T-34/76, this time a Model 1943, known in the West as the T-34/76D. This particular tank sports a mixture of rubber- and metal-rimmed road-wheels.

(*Opposite, below*) These tanks appear to be up-armoured Model 1941s. The joins in the additional armour is clearly visible on the hulls and turrets.

The commander of a T-34/76D takes a rest during a lull in the fighting.

inflated Lavrinenko's success, he had certainly shown the way with the T-34 – in the right hands it was a panzer killer.

The sheer number of T-34s produced inevitably meant that there were many other tank aces. One of Lavrinenko's nearest rivals was First Lieutenant Vladimir Alexeyevich Bochkovsky, who also fought with the 1st Guards Tank Brigade; he chalked up thirty-six kills (some of them not tanks, but other armoured fighting vehicles). He achieved his tally with both the T-34/76 and then the T-34/85.

Just behind Bochkovsky came Lieutenant M. Kuchenkov with thirty-two kills, followed by Captain N. Dyachenko, Colonel Alexander Fyodorovich Burda and N. Moiseye with thirty-one each. Burda fought in both the T-28 and the T-34/76, and eight of his kills came on one day, 4 October 1941. Captain Konstantin Mihaylovich Samohin scored thirty plus, while both Master Sergeant N. Novitsky and Major Vasiliy Yakovelich Storozhenko achieved twenty-nine (the latter fighting in the T-28, the T-34/76 and the T-34/85). Another twenty or so Red Army tank aces scored over twenty tanks and other armoured fighting vehicles apiece.

Although the T-28 medium tank was much maligned, a number of Red Army tank aces started their careers with it. As well as Burda and Storozhenko, these included Sergeant Makagon, who reportedly scored six kills with his T-28 on 22 June 1941 while serving with the 9th Tank Regiment. T-28 tanker Yevgeny A. Luppov of the 1st Guards Tank Brigade went on to score half a dozen kills in the T-34/76. Likewise Nikolay P. Kapatov started with the T-28 and then converted to the T-34/76, subsequently claiming half a dozen enemy vehicles on 6 October 1941.

Despite their obvious shortcomings, the T-34-derived self-propelled gun and tank destroyer platforms also produced a number of aces who managed to get the best out of their equipment. This was no easy feat, as these weapons were really only effective when the enemy was coming directly at them (aiming the hull-mounted gun required a lot of clutch and brake work to swing the barrel round). The 1454th Self-Propelled Artillery Regiment equipped with the SU-85 produced at least three aces who managed to knock out about half a dozen enemy tanks and self-propelled guns apiece. Sergeant Alexander Nikolayevich Kibizov, serving with the same regiment but equipped with the newer SU-100, managed to knock out twenty-four armoured fighting vehicles and countless guns.

A T-34/76B spewing out fumes from its diesel engine and kicking up the dust.

These two images clearly show the very crude finish on the T-34/85's turret. The quality of the casting and welding was much better on the earlier T-34/76.

Another photograph clearly showing the casting seams on the front of the T-34/85's turret.

Vasiliy Semyonovich Krysov fought initially with a KV-1 assigned to the 4580th Separate Heavy Tank Battalion and then with the SU-122 and the SU-85 with the 1435th and 1454th Self-Propelled Artillery Regiments, and during his career he clocked up nineteen enemy vehicles destroyed. Sergeant Nurtynov's SU-122 achieved fifteen kills, including armoured fighting vehicles and some guns.

As the commander of a heavy tank, a self-propelled gun, a tank destroyer and a T-34, Krysov fought his way westwards across Russia, Ukraine and Poland against a determined enemy – and lived to tell the tale. He wrote about his experiences after the war and these memoirs were eventually published in English.* Hitler attacked the Soviet Union the day after Krysov completed tank school, but his first battle experience came only in July 1942 when his KV-1 regiment was deployed to the important city of Kalach, on a great bend in the Don river west of Stalingrad, to prevent the German 6th Army crossing. Having fought during Operation Uranus as a KV-1 tank commander, he was later transferred to tank destroyers, commanding SU-122s and later SU-85s; he fought at Kursk and in central Ukraine, and finished the war as a T-34 commander in Germany.

Krysov recalled that he regularly came up against the Waffen-SS, including the 1st SS Leibstandarte Adolf Hitler Panzer Division in the Bruilov–Fastov area in 1943, and the 5th SS Das Wiking Panzer Division in Poland in 1944. The 1454th Self-Propelled Artillery Regiment fought with the 1st Guards Tank Army during the Battle for Lvov in the summer of 1944. At Kursk the previous year Krysov recalled facing both Panthers and Tigers, and he participated in a counterattack at Ponyri. His claim to have knocked out eight Tigers in one engagement seems rather fanciful, but perhaps reflects the tendency of all tank crews to term any type of panzer a Tiger.

Like all tank aces, these men became consummate professionals with a fatalistic outlook on life. Nonetheless, like the Red Air Force aces, they were fêted as heroes of the Motherland – and for good reason.

---

* *Panzer Destroyer: Memoirs of a Red Army Tank Commander* (Pen & Sword, 2010).

# Chapter Ten

# T-34 Killers

It is important to remember that the T-34 did not have it all its own way – far from it, as is clearly evidenced by the enormous tank losses that the Soviets suffered throughout the Second World War. Although the Red Army resurrected Marshal Tukhachevsky's concepts of Deep Battle and Deep Operation, as well as learning from the Nazi blitzkrieg, their tactics, strategy and technology all evolved as the war progressed. Following the Nazi defeats at Stalingrad and Kursk, the war on the Eastern Front became one of attrition.

Initially Nikolai Kucherenko's T-34 hull design was protected by 45mm of armour at the front, 40mm at the rear and 20mm on top. While the welding was often poor, it did not cause weld failures. At the front the glacis plate was set at 60 degrees and was free of openings apart from the driver's hatch and the ball-mounted machine gun. As a result, this gave ballistic protection of 75mm, which made the T-34 almost invulnerable in 1941. This superiority, however, was very short-lived.

The appearance of both the T-34 and the KV-1 came as a rude awakening for the panzer and anti-tank crews, who found their standard 37mm and 50mm guns could only penetrate Soviet armour at close range. The early Panzer Mk III Ausf C–Fs were armed only with a 37mm gun, while the follow-on models had a 50mm gun. The final version, the Ausf N, was armed with the short 75mm KwK L-24 anti-tank gun. This is why Panzer III chassis production was eventually switched to assault guns armed with the 75mm Stu K40 L-48. Likewise, the Panzer Mk IV only really held its own with the advent of the Ausf F2.

Once the German Army introduced the Panzer Mk IV F2 armed with the 75mm KwK 40 L-43 in May 1942 the panzers could destroy the T-34 from 1,000m rather than at point-blank range. While the Germans developed ever more deadly anti-tank weapons, the T-34's armour was less than doubled during the period 1940–1943, whereas 90mm of frontal armour was needed to offer any protection from the KwK 40. To add to the T-34 tank crews' woes, the nickel content used to harden the steel plate was very low. This meant that even if an enemy anti-tank gun did not penetrate the armour of the T-34, the violent impact could break off steel splinters that would shower the crew.

An abandoned T-34/76 Model 1941 with the 1942 cast turret. The Germans swiftly realised that they needed to develop panzers that could penetrate the T-34's armour at maximum range to compensate for their lack of numbers.

From the very start of the war the Germans possessed a weapon that was greatly feared by all Allied tankers: the 'Eighty-Eight'. Initially designed as a *Flugzeugabwehrkanone* or aircraft defence cannon, it was soon redesigned as a *Kampfwagenkanone* (or battle vehicle cannon) for the anti-tank role. Fortunately for the German forces on the Eastern Front in 1941, they found that the '88' flak gun was capable of penetrating 84mm of armour at 2,000m. In fact, this anti-aircraft gun, particularly the Flak 36, proved so successful in this dual role against tanks that it became the basis for the 88mm KwK 36 used to arm the Tiger I, while the Flak 41 evolved into both the 88mm KwK 43 for the Tiger II and the 88mm PaK 43, which was installed in the Ferdinand/Elefant, Hornisse/Nashorn (Hornet/Rhinoceros) and Jagdpanther.

The standard Germany Army anti-tank gun was the 50mm PaK 39; the scaled-up 75mm PaK 40 was introduced in 1941 and became the standard anti-tank weapon for the rest of the war. The follow-on PaK 41 could cut through 150mm of armour at 2,000m, but its squeeze-bore barrel meant it wore out quickly and increasing

An 88mm flak gun in action near a couple of wrecked T-34s. This was one of the few guns capable of penetrating the T-34's armour at range in 1941.

shortages of the tungsten required for its special ammunition ensured that only 150 were built. Another T-34 killer produced in relatively small numbers was the 88mm PaK 43/41. This was dubbed the *Scheunentor* ('barn door') by its crews because it was so heavy and difficult to manoeuvre into position. One such gun was reported to have destroyed six T-34s at a range of 3,500m, while another blew the engine out and the turret off a T-34 at a range of 500m.

Until September 1942 anti-tank guns up to and including 50mm calibre accounted for more than 75 per cent of T-34 losses, usually at very close range. In sharp contrast the 88mm accounted for only 3.4 per cent. By the summer of 1944 the 75mm and 88mm were both claiming around 40 per cent each (i.e. a total of 80 per cent) of those T-34s knocked out. During the first quarter of 1945 the 88mm was claiming up to 70 per cent. Clearly the Germans simply did not catch up with their larger calibre anti-tank guns fast enough.

The most effective T-34 killer was the Tiger I armed with the 88mm KwK 36. This had roughly a 50 per cent chance of cutting open 110mm of armour at 2,000m, while at half this range it could penetrate 138mm of armour with a 95 per cent chance of a hit. At 500m the hit probability was 100 per cent. Luckily for the T-34 crews, the Tiger I was never produced in great numbers, as it was complicated and time-consuming to build. The follow-on Tiger II with the KwK 43 gun was equally deadly – at 1,500m it had a 60 per cent chance of hitting and penetrating 148mm of armour. Once again, though, the Tiger II only appeared in very small numbers.

(*Above and opposite*) The Panzer Mk V Panther was rushed into service in the summer of 1943 as the German answer to the T-34.

(*Above and opposite*) The Tiger I was a T-34 killer that could cut through over 100mm of armour at 2,000m, but it was never produced in sufficient numbers. The T-34s simply swamped the Tigers and destroyed them at close quarters.

The German Panther was intended to be the *panzertruppen*'s answer to the T-34 and was designed to withstand the T-34's 76.2mm gun. The Germans knew that the F-34 gun could penetrate up to 63mm of armour at 1,000m. Unfortunately, while the Panther's frontal armour was as good as the Tiger's, its side armour was little better than that of the Panzer Mk IV. This meant that the Panther Ausf D and Ausf A models committed to the battles in Ukraine in 1943 were too lightly armoured. While the Ausf D had better frontal armour than the T-34/76 Model 1943, the level of protection was still inadequate. The early Panthers also suffered mechanical problems, which greatly reduced their combat availability.

The Panther was essentially a rushed design that entered combat far too quickly; nevertheless, its armament still made it an effective T-34 killer. The 75mm KwK 40 L-43 gun on the Panzer IV F2 fired an armour-piercing round that at 1,000m could penetrate 87mm of armour, therefore easily overwhelming the T-34. The gun developed for the Panther, the 75mm KwK 42 L-70, was even more powerful and could blast its way through 111mm of armour at 1,000m. This bigger gun came at a cost, though, in the shape of a bigger turret; this required a wider hull, resulting in a heavier and slower tank than was hoped for.

Hitler's 'zoo' was a range of armoured fighting vehicles and tanks equipped with various models of the 88mm – all of which could chew through the T-34. The Soviets knew that the Germans had put their faith in Hitler's 'zoo' to secure victory in 1943. Nikita Khrushchev saw captured panzer orders that confirmed as much:

> It contained a message addressed to the German troops which went something like this: 'You are now waging an offensive with tanks far superior to the Russian T-34s. Until now the T-34 has been the best tank in the world, better even than our own. But now you have our new Tiger tanks. There is no equal to them. With such a weapon you warriors of the German Army cannot fail to crush the enemy.'

'Their new tanks were very menacing indeed,' acknowledged Khrushchev, 'but our troops learned quickly how to deal with them. At Kursk we won a battle which tipped the balance of the war in our favour.'

From the air the T-34, like all tanks, was vulnerable to attack by bombers and dive-bombers. In particular, the late model Junkers Ju 87 known as the Ju 87G-1 was a conversion of the Ju 87D-5 to a dedicated tank-busting role. It was armed with a 37mm cannon beneath each wing, which was more than capable of cutting through the upper hull of the T-34.

For a period the Ju 87G-1 enjoyed some success on the Eastern Front. At Kursk the attack by the II SS Panzer Corps was aided by the Luftwaffe's *Schlachtflieger* and

The Tiger II was armed with a gun that could easily tackle the T-34s, but again it was produced in very small numbers.

A Tiger crew examine damage inflicted on their tank.

Soviet infantry take a close look at a destroyed Panther.

The Junkers Ju 87G-1 was a tank-buster armed with 37mm cannon. These aircraft were used to attack Soviet tank columns during the battle of Kursk.

The Hornet self-propelled gun married a Panzer Mk IV chassis with an 88mm anti-tank gun.

For some reason this captured T-34/76D has been mounted on a light railway, perhaps to enable it to be used as a towed pillbox.

the *Panzerjäger-Staffeln*, and the G-1s caused havoc amongst the Soviet tanks. Tactics developed by Karl Rudel, one of the top Stuka pilots, involved attacking the T-34 from behind; a direct hit on the engine would cause it to explode, destroying the tank.

On 19 July 1943 *Oberfeldwebel* Hans Krohn, a radio operator with *Stukagruppen* 3, recalled:

> Our 'cannon aircraft' took a terrible toll of Soviet armour. We attacked at very low altitude ... and my pilot opened fire at a distance of only 50 metres. Most of our attacks were made against the side of the tanks, because in that way they offered the largest targets. I know that some pilots attacked from behind because that was where the armour was weakest, but that also meant the target was so small that it was difficult to hit. By this time Soviet tank crews appeared to be well aware of the potency of our 'cannon planes'. Whenever we appeared, the tanks would start wild evasive manoeuvres. Occasionally we could see tank crews jump out of the hatches and abandon their tanks when we dived to attack them.

However, by 1943 the Stukas were increasingly being mauled by Soviet fighters, which were being produced in ever-growing numbers. Only during the opening stages of the battle of Kursk did the Germans enjoy air superiority. In addition to the Stukas, the Germans deployed the Henschel Hs 129B-2/R2 ground attack/anti-tank aircraft, which carried a 20mm cannon in the nose and a 30mm cannon mounted in a gondola beneath the fuselage. The Henschels also supported the German attack at Kursk and were used to crush a T-34 attack on the flank of the SS Panzer Corps on 8 July 1943. The Luftwaffe claimed to have destroyed 1,100 Soviet tanks at Kursk, but not all of these were as a result of the tank-buster attacks. The problem faced by the Luftwaffe was that there were never enough G-1s or R2s available to overcome the T-34 on anything other than a local level. In the face of superior Red Air Force numbers, any advantages these aircraft offered soon vanished.

Both on the ground and in the air Hitler's designers came up with some highly effective T-34 killers, but they were simply never produced in decisive numbers. In addition, the lack of standardisation greatly hampered panzer production and inevitably impacted on maintenance and tactics. While Stalin's designers also dabbled with various stopgaps and successor tanks, Soviet factories were prioritised to stick with what they knew best — namely the T-34.

# Chapter Eleven

# Cold War T-34s

Despite Hitler's defeat in Europe, the T-34 continued to see combat in the Far East throughout the closing days of the Second World War. In August 1945 it was in the forefront of the Red Army's invasion of Japanese-occupied Manchuria, which took the tanks into North Korea. The Red Army under Zhukov had fought the Japanese in Mongolia in 1939, but the subsequent truce had enabled the Soviets to concentrate on defeating the Nazis in Europe. Stalin, though, had unfinished business and his tanks simply steamrollered their way through the ill-equipped Japanese forces. The latter had nothing capable of taking on the T-34/85's armour and the Red Army cut through the Imperial Japanese Army like a knife through butter.

Quite remarkably, after the Second World War the T-34 remained in service for almost another five decades. On 25 June 1950 the North Korean People's Army attacked South Korea, its forces spearheaded by 150 Soviet-supplied T-34/85s.[*] These were superior to anything else in theatre at the time. While 120 tanks were deployed with the North Korean 105th Armoured Brigade, the North Korean infantry divisions' self-propelled gun battalions fielded a total of 120 Soviet-supplied SU-76 assault guns. In addition to the tanks of the armoured brigade, personnel from the tank training unit at Sadong, with a further thirty tanks, were assigned to the 7th Division. They deployed on the east–central front for the attack on Inje.

At first the North Koreans' T-34s rolled all before them – at least until American M26 Pershing tanks armed with a 90mm gun arrived. In the early stages of the fighting the North Koreans also used their tanks in built-up areas to some considerable effect, neutralising UN defenders. The UN forces were to dub them 'Caviar Cans'. During the assault on Taejon they moved in pairs or singly, carrying supporting infantry. Afterwards the North Koreans began to use their armour much more circumspectly because of the improving American counter-measures.

After the capture of the South Korean capital, the 105th Armoured Brigade became known as the 105th 'Seoul' Armoured Division and it was strengthened with the addition of the 308th Self-Propelled Artillery Battalion. By 1953 the North

---

[*] See the author's *Images of War: Armoured Warfare in the Korean War* (Pen & Sword, 2012).

Koreans had seven tank regiments (104th–107th, 109th, 206th and 208th). During the battles for the Pusan pocket the North Koreans received reinforcements that included another eighty T-34/85s; these equipped two new tank units, the 16th and 17th Armoured Brigades. Some were also sent to the 105th Armoured Brigade, but the UN's air supremacy meant that many were destroyed before they could reach the front. UN estimates at the end of September 1950 were that the entire North Korean T-34 force (then believed to stand at 239 tanks) had been destroyed, whereas the UN forces had lost only sixty tanks.

The Chinese People's Liberation Army enjoyed something of a windfall after the Soviet forces withdrew from Dalian on 1 December 1950. The armaments in Dalian were sold to China, including 224 T-34s and SU-100s, and 18 IS-2 heavy tanks. From these the PLA formed its 1st Mechanised Division.

After the Second World War the T-34 was also deployed to keep the Soviet bloc together. Having fought so hard to clear the Nazis from Czechoslovakia, Poland, Hungary and Romania, Stalin had no intention of relinquishing control. In 1953 T-34s were used to put down revolts against Soviet rule in East Berlin and Poland. Three years later T-34s rolled into Budapest to help crush the Hungarian rising. Although successful, the Soviets lost forty tanks during this urban battle.

During the 1956 Arab–Israeli war the Egyptian Army was equipped with 230 T-34/85s (which had come from Czechoslovakia), as well as 100 SU-100s. In the Sinai the Egyptians succumbed to superior Israeli training and equipment. Amongst the vehicles knocked out by the Israelis were twenty-six T-34/85s, one T-34 command tank and six SU-100s. Another four SU-100s were lost to the British during the fighting in the Suez area.[*] By this stage the T-34 was really obsolete but it continued to see front-line service with the Arab armies.

During the 1967 Six Day War Egyptian infantry divisions were bolstered with the T-34 and in total the Egyptians fielded about 300 of them. The fighting in the Six Day War was a disaster for the Egyptian Army, whose losses included 251 T-34/85s and 51 SU-100s. Syrian losses on the Golan Heights included seventy-three T-34/85s and seven SU-100s. This was as a result of the Israeli Army having greatly modernised its tank fleet. Despite these losses, the T-34 again saw action during the War of Attrition and the 1973 Yom Kippur War.

The T-34 also saw combat in post-colonial Africa. In 1975 Cuban troops supported by eighty T-34/85s arrived in Angola to back the Marxist MPLA against their UNITA and FNLA rivals. The T-34 served during the wars in Ethiopia, Mozambique and Somalia in the 1970s. Even in the early 1990s the T-34/85 was still in use with the Croatian and Serb Armies during the wars in the Balkans following the break-up of Yugoslavia.

---

* See the author's *Images of War: Armoured Warfare in the Arab-Israeli Conflicts* (Pen & Sword, 2013).

The T-34/85's postwar swansong came in 1950 when 150 spearheaded the North Korean invasion of South Korea.

More knocked-out North Korean T-34s. Initially the tank reigned supreme as neither the South Koreans nor their American allies had adequate anti-tank weapons.

This North Korean T-34/85 succumbed to UN air power.

(*Opposite, top*) A Soviet T-34/85 on the streets of East Berlin in June 1953 following the rising against the communist East German Government.

(*Opposite, below*) Although the Red Army crushed the Hungarian rising against communist rule in 1956, the T-34 did not have it all its own way on the streets of Budapest.

A Syrian Army Czech-built T-34/85 captured by the Israelis during the Six Day War in 1967.

A column of knocked-out Egyptian vehicles, including a T-34/85 and an SU-100, destroyed in 1967.

Mujahideen guerrillas with a T-34/85, formerly of the Afghan Army, photographed in the 1980s.

This T-34/85 belonged to the Palestinian Liberation Organisation; it was knocked out by the Israeli Air Force in Lebanon in 1982.

Bosnian Serb Army T-34/85s photographed near Doboj in early 1996. The purpose of the rubber sheets was probably to help ward off magnetic anti-tank mines.

A preserved Egyptian T-34/85 at the Egyptian National Military Museum. The T-34 enjoyed a remarkable fifty-year career, making it one of the most enduring tanks ever built.

# Epilogue
# Koshkin versus Kotin

It was two years after Mikhail Koshkin's death before Stalin and his generals finally acknowledged that he had bequeathed the Red Army something rather special. The T-34 had appeared at exactly the right moment in the Soviet Union's troubled history. While Stalin's generals told him what they thought of the tank as the war progressed, Stalin must also have remembered the engineer who was so adamant that the next medium tank needed only to run on tracks that he fatally endangered his own life to make the point.

On the eve of the Nazi invasion the Red Army had thousands of fast and light tanks, but they urgently needed an up-armoured and upgunned replacement. At the time there were just two contenders for the role: in Leningrad Zhosif Kotin and his team were working on the KV heavy tank, while in Kharkov Mikhail Koshkin and his colleagues were developing the T-34 medium tank.

The Nazis had no heavy tanks in 1940, which meant that Kotin was offering the Red Army a much-needed advantage. Kotin and his supporters argued that their heavy breakthrough tank would slice through the enemy's lines with impunity, meaning that it did not greatly matter what type of tank was used to exploit the breakthrough as the hard work had already been done. The reality was that the speed of Hitler's blitzkrieg almost sealed the fate of the KV as it was swiftly outmanoeuvred by the panzers.

What Koshkin did in the late 1930s, deliberately or not, was to create a good all-rounder that made a heavy tank largely superfluous to requirements. For Koshkin, however, in terms of design the T-34/85 was the end of the road for his creation. The SU-100 with its 100mm gun was as far as the T-34 could go with the size of its armament, and even this was far from perfect.

Kotin very nearly saw his KV consigned to the scrapheap after its poor showing in 1941. In fact, the much-maligned KV actually had much to recommend it, but it only stayed in front-line service until 1943 and only a few examples of the upgunned KV-85 were produced. In contrast, the T-34, in its various guises, fought all the way to Berlin.

Nonetheless it was Kotin who paved the way for the Soviet Union's future main battle tanks with the redesign of his KV chassis. Most notably, he produced some of the Second World War's most potent tank killers with his ISU self-propelled guns and the KV-85 and IS-1/IS-2 heavy tanks armed with massive 152mm, 85mm and 122mm guns respectively. These would eventually give rise to the T-54 and T-62, which dominated the Cold War.

Kotin's late war heavy tanks, though, were never produced in such decisive numbers as the T-34. The ISU and IS amounted to about 8,000 vehicles all told. Thanks to armaments minister Vannikov and his factories, some 60,000 T-34s of all types were built. For his part, Vannikov did such a good job for the Soviet war effort that he remained armaments minister until 1962. He was three times awarded the highest civilian honour, Hero of Socialist Labour, and twice received the State Stalin Prize first class.

In contrast, Marshal Kulik, head of the artillery directorate, almost had a catastrophic effect on the development of the T-34 and the Red Army's anti-tank defences in general. Not only did he almost derail anti-tank gun production, thanks to his harebrained scheme involving a 107mm howitzer for the T-34, he also attempted to halt the formation of dedicated anti-tank artillery brigades. By 1943 Stalin had tired of Kulik's antics and demoted him several times until he fell into obscurity.

N.N. Voronov, Kulik's deputy, had a poor opinion of his boss's abilities: 'G.I. Kulik was a poorly organised person who thought a great deal of himself and considered himself infallible. His principal method of work was to keep his subordinates in a state of fear. His favourite saying when assigning missions or giving orders was "either prison or a medal".' In contrast, Alexander Morozov, who took over from Koshkin, continued designing tanks until 1976 and the Kharkov design bureau was named after him in honour of his achievements.

Koshkin was responsible for the Soviet Union's equivalent of the American M4 Sherman, only it was much better. The T-34 took its place alongside the Sherman and the Tiger as one of the most famous and enduring tanks of the Second World War, whereas the KV and the IS tanks dwindled into obscurity. In recognition of his contribution, Mikhail Koshkin was posthumously awarded the State Stalin Prize in 1942 and the Order of the Red Star. Just before the collapse of the Soviet Union in 1990 he was posthumously decorated with the Hero of Socialist Labour. To his credit, there can be little doubt that Koshkin's legacy outlived Kotin's.

At the start of this book I stated that the T-34 won the Second World War, although this was slightly disingenuous. Soviet industry also won the war, along with Koshkin and his team, who designed a tank that Soviet factories could churn out at a massive rate. In fact, the numbers seem so astonishing as to be literally unbelievable, and no doubt they are tainted by postwar Soviet propaganda. There is no real way of verifying the enormous numbers of T-34s produced but the actual figures, in truth, are immaterial – what is important is that the Soviets produced more tanks than the Germans could knock out.

It should also be borne in mind that while the Germans produced many T-34 tank killers, another enemy of the T-34 was quality control. The sheer scale of output meant that quality was sacrificed. Tanks were often rushed into battle straight from the factories; Red Army tank losses were such that replacements had to be shipped immediately to the front. For both the battle of Moscow and the siege of Stalingrad, they were driven out of the factory doors and into battle.

The Paton welding system, and the haste with which it was used, meant that the quality of the welding was often poor; while this did not result in widespread structure failure, inevitably some welds would have fractured on impact with an anti-tank round. In the early models the diesel engines and transmission units could be notoriously temperamental. The lack of dedicated armoured recovery vehicles for the T-34 often meant that tanks that became stranded or broke down in combat simply had to be abandoned until the fighting was over. This expedient, of course, only worked if you were left in possession of the battlefield. In addition, the tank could only be as good as the men handling it, and the lack of organisation and proficient training in the summer of 1941 meant that any advantage the T-34 had was simply thrown away.

While the Germans produced some excellent anti-tank guns, tanks and self-propelled guns that were more than capable of tackling the T-34, in the summer of 1943, which proved to be the turning point in the war on the Eastern Front, they were simply not available in sufficient numbers. For example, 1,750 Panther tanks were built in 1943, although only 1,071 reached the front. Just 647 Tiger Is were built in 1943, along with 345 Rhinoceros and 90 Ferdinand self-propelled guns. Just over 3,000 Panzer IVs and 3,000 StuG IIIs armed with the L-43 or L-48 were produced. Compare these figures to the 15,812 T-34s built in 1943, including 283 T-34/85s (plus another 4,047 assault guns, 3,463 light tanks and 684 heavy tanks); in the previous year they had produced 12,553 T-34/76s.

In 1943 Soviet tank losses of all types outstripped even the disasters of 1941 with 22,400 tanks destroyed, while the Germans lost 6,362 on all fronts. The following year the Red Army lost another 16,900 tanks, compared with panzer losses of 6,434. This did not matter because Soviet tank production peaked in 1944 at 28,983 (including 14,773 T-34s); given its huge numerical advantage, the T-34 was unstoppable.

By 1943 the Germans were being outproduced by almost 3:1. Rather than disrupt tank production, the Soviet high command put off introducing a successor to the T-34/76 until it truly became necessary. In contrast, the Germans diverted 41 per cent of their tank-producing capabilities to the Tiger and the Panther at the expense of the Panzer IV, which actually remained the backbone of the panzer units. As a result, not enough tanks reached the depleted panzer units. It proved to be a strategic gamble, and Stalin won. Even in 1944, when the panzer factories pulled out all the stops, they were still outproduced by 2:1 and the following year was even worse at 4:1.

The four key design features accounting for the T-34's success were the sloping armour, (initially) a bigger gun than the panzers, a diesel engine and wide tracks. By the time the Germans attempted to emulate this formula, it was all but too late. The fact that the T-34 continued to see combat into the 1990s is testimony to its durability. The T-34 was no wonder weapon, but it was good and it just happened to be in the right place at the right time. It proved to be what Stalin and the Red Army needed – a true war winner.

# Further Reading

Bevan, Tim and Fowler, Will, *Russian Tanks of World War II. Stalin's Armoured Might* (Ian Allen, 2002)

Ellis, Chris, *Tanks of World War II* (Chancellor Press, 1997)

Ellis, Chris and Chamberlain, Peter, *The Great Tanks* (Hamlyn, 1975)

Forczyk, Robert, *Panther vs T-34, Ukraine 1943* (Osprey Publishing Ltd, 2007)

Healy, Mark, *Kursk 1943. The tide turns in the East* (Osprey Publishing Ltd, 2002)

Hughes, Dr Matthew and Mann, Dr Chris, *The T-34 Tank* (Spellmount Ltd, 1999)

Miller, David, *The Illustrated Directory of Tanks of the World from World War I to the Present Day* (Greenwich Editions, 2005)

Milsom, John and Zaloga, Steven, *Russian Tanks of World War 2* (Patrick Stephens, 1977)

Zaloga, Steven, *Bagration 1944. The Destruction of Army Group Centre* (Osprey Publishing Ltd, 1999)